DATE DUE

DE 4 00			
DE 1 01			
1 2 00			
MY 2 0 10			

DEMCO 38-296

The Politics of
Prison Expansion

The Politics of Prison Expansion

WINNING ELECTIONS BY WAGING WAR ON CRIME

Joseph Dillon Davey

 PRAEGER

Westport, Connecticut
London

Library of Congress Cataloging-in-Publication Data

Davey, Joseph Dillon.
    The politics of prison expansion : winning elections by waging war
on crime / Joseph Dillon Davey.
        p.   cm.
    Includes bibliographical references and index.
    ISBN 0–275–96209–1 (alk. paper)
    1. Imprisonment—United States—States.   2. Rhetoric—Political
aspects—United States—States.   3. Governors—United States.
4. Governors—United States—Election.   I. Title.
HV9471.D37   1998
365'.973—dc21   97–49278

British Library Cataloguing in Publication Data is available.

Library of Congress Catalog Card Number: 97–49278
ISBN: 0–275–96209–1

First published in 1998

Praeger Publishers, 88 Post Road West, Westport, CT 06881
An imprint of Greenwood Publishing Group, Inc.

Printed in the United States of America

The paper used in this book complies with the
Permanent Paper Standard issued by the National
Information Standards Organization (Z39.48–1984).

10 9 8 7 6 5 4 3 2 1

To Linda DuBois Davey, and our grandchildren,
Nolan, Christian, Noelle, Kellen, the Davey-Beatty twins,
and all those to come in the future. Pop loves you.

Contents

Tables

Acknowledgments

I would like to thank Professor Frances Fox Piven and Professor John Mollenkopf of the Graduate Center of the City University of New York for all of their help in the writing of this book. Without their guidance and encouragement, this work would never have been completed.

Linda DuBois Davey once again functioned as my main editor. In addition to patiently reading every word of every draft of this work and pointing out the incomprehensible wording of some sections and inconsistencies in some of my arguments, she also listened attentively and questioned thoughtfully as the ideas expressed herein were taking shape. If the readers of this work benefit from my research in any way, they owe Linda much of the credit.

For her assistance, her encouragement, her patience and her support, I will forever be in her debt.

Introduction

In the last two decades there has been an unprecedented increase in the use of imprisonment in the United States. This expansion in the imprisonment rate did not happen in the other Western democracies and, more important, it happened very unevenly among the fifty U.S. states. The increase in imprisonment rates per 100,000 population among the fifty states between 1972 and 1992 ranged from a low of 55 percent in West Virginia to a high of 690 percent in Delaware. Why was there such variation in the rate of increase in imprisonment among the fifty states? Was it associated with increased rates of reported crime in each state? Are there socioeconomic variables that may increase the likelihood of rapid prison growth? Are there political factors that influence these increases?

The literature on the subject of variations in imprisonment patterns is limited. Three theories have been offered to explain the growth of imprisonment rates. The first could be called the "Durkheim-Blumstein" tradition, the second is the "Marxist-Rusche and Kircheimer" tradition, and the third is the "racial bias" theory. The first argues that a society's crime rate determines its imprisonment rate; the second argues that economic factors are more salient for imprisonment rates than a society's crime levels; the third suggests that the war on crime is really a thinly veiled war on African-Americans.

However, the increases in the levels of imprisonment in the fifty states between 1972 and 1992 cannot be explained by any one of these theories alone, nor by all of them together. I correlated the rate of imprisonment increase in the fifty states with the increase in the crime rate in those states and then with six other socioeconomic variables that researchers often associate with high imprisonment rates. The correlational coefficients were so low that a further investigation of the causes of the variation was clearly warranted.

Therefore, from a list of states that had high rates of increase in imprisonment, states with imprisonment rate increases greater than any of their neighbors were selected from six different regions of the United States. The governor who had presided over the most rapid increase in the imprisonment rate in those states was identified. Then, that governor's political views and rhetoric concerning crime and punishment were analyzed, and the views and rhetoric of contemporaneous governors of contiguous states that did not experience rapid growth in imprisonment were analyzed as well.

My view is that neither crime rates nor any other socioeconomic variables are important in explaining the variations in the rate of imprisonment expansion, but that the practice of "law and order" politics by individual governors is important. Moreover, while both formal and informal processes are at work in prison expansion, the informal processes may well be the more significant.

Prison expansion has been neither an outgrowth of unusual increases in crime nor an effective method of reducing further increases. However, "waging war on crime" has indeed been a very effective method of winning gubernatorial elections.

1

The Puzzle of Imprisonment Increases

THE IMPRISONMENT EXPLOSION FROM 1972 TO 1992

The last three decades of the twentieth century saw the most dramatic growth of incarceration rates in American history. Prisons in the United States contained around 196,000 inmates in 1972, yet by 1992, the population exceeded 846,000.[1] Jails in the United States experienced comparable growth during this period; consequently, in the United States the combined incarceration rate per 100,000 population in 1992 stood at 504,[2] the highest in the world[3] and more than five times the incarceration rate of any Western European nation.[4]

This dramatic growth happened despite the fact that almost every knowledgeable observer of the criminal justice system agrees that incarceration is an expensive undertaking that probably does little to reduce crime. For example, a study by Isaac Erhlich on the effects of incarceration estimated that if the time served by the average prison inmate were cut in half, we could expect no more than a 5 percent increase in serious offenses.[5] More recently, a study by the Rand Corporation's Criminal Justice Program "showed that prevention programs were dramatically more effective in terms of cost per crime prevented" than the new "three strikes laws" that seem to be popular with political candidates.[6]

The cost in tax dollars of present incarceration policies is rarely discussed by political leaders but very often shocks the casual observer. Actually, the annual cost of keeping an inmate in prison varies from state to state, but one authority has said that "a conservative estimate is $25,000 in yearly operating costs per inmate," with a construction cost of $70,000 to $100,000 per cell.[7] State spending on correctional activities was $1.3 billion (in unadjusted dollars) in 1972;[8] by 1992, the last year for which figures are available, the cost was $31.4 billion.[9] However, even in inflation-adjusted dollars, between 1980 and 1992, the per capita cost of corrections in the United States rose by 306.2 percent.[10]

In 1996, there were over 1.5 million people behind bars in the United States, and the numbers continue to grow. There is something of a construction boom going on in the prisons. The federal government constructed twenty-six new federal prisons in 1996, while the states were constructing ninety-five new prisons. The total number of new prison beds created in 1996 was around 104,000, and the total cost of the construction was in the area of $7 billion.[11]

However, there may be even more rapid growth in controlling offenders through electronic monitoring and house arrest, known now as computer-assisted monitoring of offenders (CAMO). According to one CAMO authority, this type of social control "is in its infancy and may become the single most significant sentencing and correctional alternative of the twenty-first century. Currently, there may be as many as seventy thousand offenders under some form of CAMO control and this number may well triple by the year 2000."[12] Since the cost of CAMO is a fraction of incarceration (and, in fact, frequently paid for by the offender), there is a great temptation to expand these programs.

The trend toward greater punitiveness appears to be not only growing, but becoming more bipartisan. President Bill Clinton's 1996 crime bill stiffened mandatory sentences, created "trust funds" to build more prisons, allowed juveniles to be treated as adults for purposes of criminal prosecution and extended the death penalty to fifty-two new crimes,[13] Herbert Gans, who concentrates his research on poverty rather than crime policy, has noted the new bipartisan attitude toward greater punitiveness. Gans recently observed that "policies to eliminate street crime and related threats to personal safety are as old as the hills, and the Clinton administration has set in motion a new spasm of increased punishments, longer prison sentences and prison building."[14]

The ultimate example of the current punitiveness is the recent spate of three strikes laws, which generally mandate a sentence of life in prison without possibility of parole for a third felony conviction. Jerome Skolnick has observed that these laws probably will "only serve to increase the public's fear of crime."[15] Others have noted the irony of "getting tough" with older criminals since the "three-time losers are at the verge of aging out of crime, anyway"; since they are at the end of their offending career the three strikes laws will do very little to reduce crime.[16]

Perhaps the epitome of the potential effect of three strikes laws was exemplified in a recent California case. "On March 2, 1995, Jerry Dewayne Williams, a California man who had four prior felony convictions, was sentenced to a term of 25 years to life for stealing a slice of pizza from some children."[17] California taxpayers may have to spend a million dollars to incarcerate Williams, notwithstanding the fact that he was not likely to commit any kind of violent offense had he remained free.

To put some perspective on the current trend toward greater punitiveness, there are more than five times as many individuals behind bars in the United States today as there were when Richard Nixon left office. This is true even though only 27 out of every 100 individuals admitted to prison last year were convicted of a violent crime. If the sentencing policies that have brought about this glut of inmates can be justified, it must be by showing that either the crime rate had increased so much that it became necessary to do something about it or by demonstrating solid evidence that increasing incarceration reduces crime rates. A look at North and South Dakota may be informative in this area.

THE UNUSUAL TALE OF THE DAKOTAS

In 1991, criminologists James Austin and John Irwin compared the crime and imprisonment rates of North and South Dakota.[18] What they observed led me to the question raised by this volume. North and South Dakota have very similar rates of crime. The rate of crime reported to police is about 3 percent higher in South Dakota than it is in North Dakota (in 1992, there were 2,903 index crimes per 100,000 population in North Dakota and 2,998 in South Dakota; the national average in 1992 was about 5,200).[19] (Note: "index crimes" are reported in the Uniform Crime Reports and consist of homicide, rape, robbery, aggravated assault, burglary, larceny and car theft.)

However, the rate of imprisonment in the two states is very different. In fact, in 1996 South Dakota had more than three times as many prisoners per 1,000 population as North Dakota. In other words, for every 1,000 crimes reported to the police, South Dakota was around three times more likely to incarcerate someone than North Dakota.

This was not always the case. In 1972 it was also true that each state had roughly the same crime rate (1,987 index crimes reported per 100,000 population in North Dakota and 2,127 in South Dakota). However, in 1972 the rate of imprisonment in the two states was much closer than it is today. (North Dakota had 28.8 inmates per 100,000 population; South Dakota had 51.0.)

In the last twenty years both states have increased their rate of imprisonment, but at dramatically different rates. Between 1972 and 1992, South Dakota increased its imprisonment rate over 300 percent, so that today, the rate of imprisonment per 100,000 population (208) is more than triple that of North Dakota (67). What were the variables associated with the different rates of increase in incarceration in these two neighboring states? Why is it that, at least in the Dakotas, there seems to be no association

Table 1.1
States with the Highest and Lowest Imprisonment Rate Increases per 100,000
Population between 1972 and 1992

PERCENTAGE INCREASE IN:

	IMPRISONMENT RATE	UCR RATE
Delaware	690%	4,848
Alaska	535%	5,569
New York	432%	5,858
Arizona	430%	7,028
Louisiana	423%	6,546
New Hampshire	420%	3,080
Vermont	401%	3,410
Massachusetts	400%	5,002
AVG. OF HIGH STATES	466%	5,168
Minnesota	150%	4,590
Washington	150%	6,172
Nebraska	140%	4,324
North Dakota	130%	2,903
Georgia	110%	6,405
Oregon	105%	5,820
North Carolina	82%	5,802
West Virginia	55%	2,609
AVG. OF LOW STATES	115%	4,828

UCR = FBI's *Uniform Crime Reports* data.

Source: Adapted by Joseph Dillon Davey from U.S. Department of Justice, *Sourcebook of Criminal Justice Statistics 1993* (Washington, D.C.: Bureau of Justice Statistics, 1994).

between increases in the crime level and increases in the imprisonment rate? If prisons are effective, then why have crime rates not fallen in South Dakota or soared in North Dakota? Does the experience in the Dakotas hold up in a fifty-state data set for the twenty years between 1972 and 1992? Do other social variables have salience for prison expansion?

To begin my inquiry, I looked at the rate of imprisonment per 100,000 population for all fifty states and noted that there was significant variation, most of it along regional lines (the South generally has the highest rates of imprisonment). Second, I noted that all fifty states experienced substantial increases in their levels of imprisonment during this time period, but at very different rates. The difference in the rate of increase of imprisonment in the Dakotas was actually a lot less than the differences between many other states. In fact, as can be seen in Table 1.1, Delaware's rate of increase was thirteen times the rate of increase in West Virginia. Why would one state increase the rate of imprisonment per capita thirteen times faster (over a twenty-year period) than a second state with similar patterns of crime?

My initial inquiry was to determine if this variation in the rate of increase in imprisonment was associated with the variation in the rate of reported crime in these states. First, I examined the data from the states with the highest and lowest rates of increase in imprisonment. Table 1.1 lists the eight states with the highest increase in imprisonment and the eight states with the lowest increase. The former group averaged an increase of 462 percent in their rate of imprisonment, and the latter group averaged an increase that was less than one-fourth the rate of high-increase states (viz., 110 percent).

Did one group have a significantly different rate of crime? The FBI's *Uniform Crime Reports* (UCR) is the only source of national crime data that is disaggregated on the state level. According to the UCR, the eight "highest increase states" (shown in Table 1.1) have an average crime rate per 100,000 population of 5,167. However, the eight "lowest increase states" have an average of 4,823, which is only 7 percent lower. In other words, the initial impression from the data is that there seems to be little association between imprisonment increases and the overall crime problem. Like North and South Dakota, the sixteen states on the extreme ends of the imprisonment increase chart show little difference in crime rates.

If the problem of crime does not differ much between the states with the greatest prison expansion and the states with the smallest, then why, between 1972 and 1992, did some states increase their imprisonment rate by as much as thirteen times the increase in low-increase states? In other words, what has been the driving force behind the extraordinary prison expansion of the last quarter-century, and will an examination of the staggering variation in rates of growth among the states provide clues to the answer?

OVERVIEW

The literature in this field is limited. Generally, three theses have been advanced to explain variations in the use of prisons. Chapter 2 examines the work of Marxist theorists, "social control" theorists and theories on racial bias and imprisonment. Most of the research data that support these theories is dated, and all three theories appear to leave unanswered many questions concerning the rapid expansion of imprisonment in recent decades.

In Chapter 3 the association between the increase in the rate of imprisonment and the increase in the rate of crime is examined. The assumption made in the Durkheim-Blumstein thesis, that crime and imprisonment are closely associated, is tested. Chapter 4 examines the correlational coefficients between imprisonment rate increases and several other social and economic variables. Are the "usual suspects" (i.e, poverty, race, drug arrests, homicide rates, unemployment) salient to explain the growing rates of imprisonment?

Both Chapters 3 and 4 draw a bivariate correlation and a multiple regression analysis of the increases in the rate of imprisonment per 100,000 population in the fifty states between 1972 and 1992, on the one hand, and those variables that are suggested by the three theories in the literature, on the other. It is apparent from the data in these two chapters that the suspected social and economic variables offer, at best, only an incomplete explanation of the variations in imprisonment expansion.

Chapter 3 provokes the question of how the U.S. prison population more than quadrupled in a twenty-year period in the absence of any comparable changes in the crime rate without prompting scholarly research into why and how this happened? Chapter 4 suggests that many of the socioeconomic variables usually associated with high crime rates did not vary greatly between the states that rapidly increased the imprisonment rates and those that did not.

The role that politics played in causing states to increase their imprisonment rates has been largely ignored in the literature. The most active researchers in this field, Zimring and Hawkins, discussed this issue and concluded, "Surprisingly little is known about the factors that influence the size of a prison system, or the degree to which the scale of imprisonment may be expected to change over time."[20]

Despite the fact that the cost of building and operating U.S. prisons has reached levels that would have been unimaginable two decades ago, the index to the *Journal of Political Economy* lacks any reference to articles on the determinants of the scale of imprisonment.[21] Zimring and Hawkins refer to this problem by saying that "in the present state of knowledge there are no answers to questions of this kind and we can only speculate because the necessary research has not yet been done."[22]

There has never been a study on such things as "the election of a law-and-order state government"[23] or that government's influence on the state's prison population.[24] Chapter 5 undertakes such a study by looking at the increases in imprisonment rates that are associated with the "law and order" politics of various governors, as well as the absence of such increases in contiguous states during the same period.

Taken together, Chapters 5 and 6 contain the crux of my argument. The importance of the positions concerning crime and punishment taken by governors is analyzed in Chapter 5. The formal and informal processes that bring about rapid prison expansion are analyzed in Chapter 6, and Chapter 7 discusses the probable future of prison expansion.

METHODOLOGY

This work seeks to examine a previously ignored variable in the explanation of prison expansion, that of politics. The particular subject is the "law and order" politics of the governors who have presided over the largest expansion of the imprisonment rate in the recent past. I have compared the political rhetoric and policies regarding the problem of crime and punishment offered by these governors and contrasted them to those of their counterparts in contiguous states. In so doing, I have sought to evaluate the role of politics in bringing about prison expansion.

Why Governors?

There is no question that many political leaders other than governors can influence the rate of imprisonment. Public opinion polls have indicated that public awareness of the problems of crime and illegal drugs escalated quickly after President George Bush launched his "war on drugs" in the late 1980s. By drawing voters' attention to the crime problem, political leaders at any level can arouse fear that will translate into greater public demands for harsher penalties.

However, it is my argument that state political leaders most significantly influence the growth in imprisonment rates. Even when the crime rate, changes in the crime rate over time, or other socioeconomic variables are similar in two comparable states, differences in the growth of imprisonment in those two states can still be enormous. My argument is that the differences among the states in the rate of prison expansion are rooted in the political atmosphere in each state regarding the appropriate treatment of criminal offenders.

Federal, city and county governments have little to do with state prisons. These prisons are built, operated and funded by state governments, and they contain inmates who have violated state penal codes. Moreover, so much discretion is generally given to criminal justice officials in their dealings with offenders that their attitudes concerning the value of imprisonment can be very important in determining the number of individuals sent to prison in a particular state.

This study contends that the attitude of criminal justice officials toward the use of imprisonment can be strongly influenced by the views expressed by political leaders. A governor who wants to encourage a Draconian approach to the problem of crime can send out a law-and-order message to participants in the state criminal justice system and expect a quick response. For instance, parole officers can instantly toughen their policies regarding when to "violate" parolees and return them to prison for minor infractions. Probation officers ordinarily need judicial approval to incarcerate a probationer, but the discretion they exercise in this regard is also significant. Deputy district attorneys (DAs) can take a harder line in negotiating pleas; judges can opt for the harsher sentencing options given them by the law. Similarly, police officers can exercise their discretion and make a formal arrest instead of giving a warning.

Part of the argument made here is that rapid prison expansion does not necessarily require formal legislative changes. While formal changes in elements such as the state penal code or prison construction authorizations can contribute to a long-term growth of imprisonment rates, "informal" policy changes regarding the exercise of discretion over the treatment of offenders can very quickly impact the rate of imprisonment in a state. Since that discretion can be significantly influenced by the political rhetoric of law-and-order governors, the rhetoric of these governors is worth analyzing and contrasting with the rhetoric of their counterparts in neighboring states.

It may be that these governors actually believe their own rhetoric concerning law-and-order campaigns; however, whether they believe it or not, as a political strategem it has been remarkably useful.

Which Governors?

The U.S. Justice Department has been keeping records of the rate of imprisonment per 100,000 population in each of the fifty states since 1972. In order to determine if there is an identifiable association between the increase in the rate of imprisonment in state prisons and the political views of governors, the first task is to identify states that had a very dramatic growth in imprisonment rates. Since there are pronounced regional differences in the use of imprisonment, it is advisable to select different regions of the country for analysis. From these different regions, those states with the biggest increases can be singled out from the Justice Department records and contrasted with comparable states in the same region.

Table 1.2 shows the twenty-five states with imprisonment increases between 1972 and 1992 that were above the national median; Table 1.3 shows states below the median. By identifying states from the same region with substantial variations in imprisonment rate increase, it may be possible to locate causes of imprisonment increase while holding constant regional, demographic, social and economic variables.

Table 1.4 lists six "high-increase states" from six different regions of the nation and six contiguous states that can serve as "control states." The regions chosen for this study are the Northeast, the Middle Atlantic, Appalachia, the South, the Midwest and the West. From each region a state was chosen that showed the highest rate of increase in imprisonment and a contiguous state with a lower rate than any of the other neighbors was chosen as a control.

Since the growth of imprisonment rates in the high-increase states appears, in every case, to come in episodic spurts over the twenty years rather than a steady, even increase, it is possible to find the four-year period wherein the most rapid growth was recorded and (obviously) to identify the governor who presided over that growth. Each of the states selected would have had five gubernatorial administrations during the twenty years

Table 1.2
The Twenty-Five States with the Highest Imprisonment Rate Increases per
100,000 Population between 1972 and 1992

		% INCREASE IN INCARCERATION
1.	DE	690
2.	AK	435
3.	IL	435
4.	AZ	430
5.	NY	430
6.	LA	423
7.	NH	420
8.	VT	401
9.	MA	400
10.	RI	370
11.	MT	355
12.	OH	350
13.	CT	349
14.	MI	340
15.	HI	325
16.	AR	325
17.	ID	320
18.	MO	320
19.	SD	305
20.	CA	305
21.	NJ	301
22.	SC	300
23.	MS	295
24.	AL	294
25.	PA	293
	AVERAGE INCREASE	368%

Source: Adapted by Joseph Dillon Davey from U.S. Department of Justice, *Sourcebook of Criminal Justice Statistics, 1993* (Washington, D.C.: Bureau of Justice Statistics, 1994).

between 1972 and 1992. The chosen governor was the one who presided over the biggest increase in the rate of inmates per 100,000 population.

For example, Kentucky had five gubernatorial terms between 1972 and 1992. The first governor presided over an increase in imprisonment rates of about 11 per 100,000 population during the four years of his term. Another Kentucky governor saw an increase of 5 per 100,000; a third saw about 20; and a fourth, about 22. However, between 1988 and 1992, the increase in imprisonment in Kentucky was 115 per 100,000 population. Therefore, it would be reasonable to compare the political views concerning crime and punishment of the governor who presided over that increase and compare those views to those of his or her counterpart in a low-growth, demographically comparable, contiguous state, such as West Virginia.

Another example is Delaware. The increase in Delaware's imprisonment rate was 690 percent over the twenty-year period. The largest increase during any single gubernatorial administration came during the tenure of Governor Michael Castle, between 1985 and 1989. The increase of 68 inmates

Table 1.3
The Twenty-Five States with the Lowest Imprisonment Rate Increases per
100,000 Population between 1972 and 1992

	% INCREASE IN INCARCERATION
26. WI	290
27. NV	270
28. NM	253
29. IA	251
30. IN	235
31. OK	228
32. KS	225
33. CO	215
34. KY	210
35. VA	207
36. WY	200
37. TN	185
38. UT	185
39. MD	175
40. ME	162
41. TX	153
42. FL	155
43. MN	150
44. WA	150
45. NE	140
46. ND	130
47. GA	110
48. OR	105
49. NC	82
50. WV	55
AVERAGE INCREASE	181%

Source: Adapted by Joseph Dillon Davey from U.S. Department of Justice, *Sourcebook of Criminal Justice Statistics, 1993* (Washington, D.C.: Bureau of Justice Statistics, 1994).

per 100,000 population was the biggest increase in Delaware's imprisonment rate of any of the five gubernatorial administrations between 1972 and 1992.

In New Hampshire the rate of imprisonment grew every year between 1972 and 1992, for a total increase of 125 inmates per 100,000 population. However, in a single four-year period, under the governorship of Judd Gregg, the growth was 54 inmates per 100,000. Moreover, in neighboring Maine, during the contemporaneous governorship of John McKernan, the rate of imprisonment remained completely unchanged. Gregg, as we shall see, was a strong advocate of law and order; McKernan was not.

In addition to the high-increase states of New Hampshire, Delaware and Kentucky, the states of South Carolina, Missouri and Arizona show the highest rate of increase in imprisonment in their respective region during the 1972 to 1992 period. Therefore, the analysis here will be of the gubernatorial administrations that presided over the largest four-year increase

Table 1.4
States Chosen for This Study

REGION	HIGH GROWTH STATE	LOW GROWTH STATE	TIME PERIOD
NEW ENGLAND	NEW HAMPSHIRE	MAINE	1989-1993
MIDWEST	MISSOURI	KANSAS	1989-1993
THE SOUTH	SOUTH CAROLINA	NORTH CAROLINA	1988-1992
MID-ATLANTIC	DELAWARE	MARYLAND	1985-1989
APPALACHIA	KENTUCKY	WEST VIRGINIA	1986-1990
THE WEST	ARIZONA	AZ NEIGHBORS	1987
		(CALIFORNIA, UTAH, NEVADA AND NEW MEXICO)	

in imprisonment in these states between 1972 and 1992 and contemporaneous gubernatorial administrations in contiguous, low-increase states.

Specifically, the states and the years involved can be seen in Table 1.4. The specific governors who occupied the statehouse in each of these states during this period can be seen in Table 1.5.

As an afterthought, I was curious to see if any differences could be found in growth rates between the state with the highest rate of imprisonment and the state with the lowest rate. In the last year for which the information is available, the state with the highest rate of imprisonment in the United States was Louisiana and the state with the lowest rate was North Dakota. Therefore, the Louisiana governor who presided over the most rapid increase in imprisonment is compared to the contemporaneous North Dakota governor, even though there are marked demographic, social and economic differences between the two states.

Table 1.5
Governors of the States in This Study

STATE	GOVERNOR	TERM	INCREASE IN IMPRISONMENT RATE
New Hampshire	Judd Gregg	1989-1993	+54
Maine	John McKernan		+00
Missouri	John Ashcroft	1989-1993	+75
Kansas	Joan Finney		+06
S. Carolina	Carroll Campbell	1986-1990	+42
N. Carolina	James G.Martin		-02
Delaware	Michael Castle	1985-1989	+68
Maryland	William Schaeffer		+06
Kentucky	Wallace Wilkinson	1987-1991	+99
W.Virginia	Gaston Caperton		+09
Arizona*	Evan Mecham	1987	+39
CA, UT, NV, NM, CO, ID		(average)	+11
Louisiana	Buddy Roemer	1988-1992	+116
North Dakota	George Sinner		+11

*In the case of Arizona, the governor was impeached after just fourteen months of his term. Nonetheless, in that brief period Arizona experienced an unprecedented growth of imprisonment. Because the time period of the comparison is short, I have compared Arizona's prison growth with the prison growth of all its neighbors.

NOTES

1. U.S. Department of Justice, *Sourcebook of Criminal Justice Statistics, 1994* (Washington, D.C.: Bureau of Justice Statistics, 1995), p. 540.

2. Ibid., p. 533.

3. Eric Juzenas, "Prevention: Best Approach to Public Health Threat of Violence," *Nation's Health* 26 (January 1, 1996): 12.

4. James A. Inciardi, *Criminal Justice*, 5th ed. (New York: Harcourt Brace College Publishers, 1996), p. 595.

5. Isaac Erhlich, "Participation in Illegitimate Activities: An Economic Analysis," *Journal of Political Economy* 81 (1973): 521–567. See also David Greenberg, "The Incapacitative Effect of Imprisonment: Some Estimates," *Law and Society Review* 9 (Summer 1975): 541–580.

6. Juzenas, "Prevention," p. 12.

7. Elliot Currie, *Reckoning: Drugs, the Cities and the American Future* (New York: Hill and Wang, 1993), p. 152.

8. U.S. Department of Justice, *Sourcebook of Criminal Justice Statistics, 1991* (Washington, D.C.: Bureau of Justice Statistics, 1992), p. 22.

9. U.S. Department of Justice, *Sourcebook of Criminal Justice Statistics, 1994*, p. 4.

10. Ibid., p. 11.

11. *USA Today*, March 13, 1996, p. A3.

12. William G. Archambeault, "Impact of Computer Based Technologies on Criminal Justice," in Roslyn Muraskin and Albert R. Roberts, eds., *Visions for Change: Crime and Justice in the Twenty-First Century* (Upper Saddle River, N.J.: Prentice-Hall, 1996), p. 307.

13. James Ridgeway, "Bill to Cities: Lock 'Em Up," *Village Voice*, February 22, 1994, pp. 13–14.

14. Herbert Gans, *The War against the Poor: The Underclass and Antipoverty Policy* (New York: Basic Books, 1995), p. 104.

15. Jerome Skolnick, "Wild Pitch: 'Three Strikes You're Out' and Other Bad Calls on Crime," *American Prospect* 17 (Spring 1994): 30–37.

16. RAND Corporation, "California's New Three Strikes Law: Benefits, Costs and Alternatives," RAND Research Brief (Santa Monica, Calif.: RAND Corporation, 1994).

17. "Three Strikes Term for Pizza Thief in California," *Boston Globe*, March 3, 1995, p. 3.

18. James Austin and John Irwin, *Who Goes to Prison?* (San Francisco: National Council on Crime and Delinquency, 1991).

19. See Appendixes 1 and 3 for the crime and imprisonment figures on North and South Dakota.

20. Franklin E. Zimring and Gordon Hawkins, *Incapacitation: Penal Confinement and the Restraint of Crime* (New York: Oxford University Press, 1995), p. 168.

21. Franklin E. Zimring and Gordon Hawkins, *The Scale of Imprisonment* (Chicago: University of Chicago Press, 1991), p. 215.

22. Ibid., p. 114.

23. Herbert Jacob, *The Frustration of Policy: Responses to Crime by American Cities* (Boston: Little, Brown, 1984), p. 209.

24. Zimring and Hawkins, *The Scale of Imprisonment*, p. 114.

2

Review of the Literature on Imprisonment Growth

The literature on crime offers three currents of thought on the subject of changing incarceration levels. One suggests a "constancy of punishment"[1] and has been referred to as "the Durkheim-Blumstein perspective."[2] In this view, criminal law and the legal process are seen as reactively punishing individuals in relation to the amount of crime that occurs. While this theory is probably the most common and the most intuitive perspective, we shall see from the data on crime and imprisonment that this view is, at best, just a partial explanation of the changes in incarceration levels over the last three decades.

The second view can be considered a Marxist perspective, which asserts "that incarceration rates are influenced by the fluctuating needs of dominant elites to maintain social control."[3] Marxist theorists assert that punishments are meted out in relation to changes in levels of economic inequality. However, this perspective, also, is very difficult to reconcile with recent changes.

A third perspective has most recently been summarized by Michael Tonry. It suggests that the rapid increases in imprisonment levels in the recent past is an outgrowth of the war on drugs, which is, in fact, a thinly disguised war on African-Americans. However, although doubtless there is some merit in this argument, it can explain just a fraction of the overall changes that have been made.

MARXIST PERSPECTIVE

It has been argued that "there is no Marxist theory of deviance."[4] Marx himself, of course, said very little about the subject of crime and never advanced a theory concerning the severity of penal practices.[5] The earliest appearance of a Marxist view was in *Punishment and Social Structure* (1939) by Georg Rusche and Otto Kircheimer, which has been called "the landmark Marxist account of the nexus between the economy and social control."[6]

Rusche and Kircheimer offer a historical analysis from the end of the sixteenth century to the 1930s, in which they assert that labor market demands and conditions were what governed the use of imprisonment during that time. They outline the history of penal systems, which they view as a series of epochs in which the different penal systems are closely related to phases of economic development. By introducing the idea that imprisonment is a function of the larger social structure, and not of crime, they thereby broke from traditional criminal justice theory. In effect, they were saying that the societal response to crime is not a simple consequence of crime itself.[7]

Research on the Rusche and Kirchheimer Theory

Numerous researchers have argued that unemployment rates predict increases in incarceration independent of increases in crime.[8] In 1978 Dario Melossi noted that Rusche and Kirchheimer had been ignored for many years until the recent "rediscovery of the classic."[9] A decade later Melossi expanded on this theme in *The State of Social Control*, where he concluded that imprisonment was, in fact, used to establish the discipline and management of labor.

David Greenberg did a series of studies between 1975 and 1981 that were based on Rusche and Kirchheimer's work. Greenberg offered an interpretation of changes in the size of prison populations according to which "the oscillatory behavior of imprisonment rates is attributed to oscillations in unemployment."[10] He later concluded that "when the supply of labor is high relative to demand, this perspective would suggest that the rate of imprisonment would be increased, with the goal of taking excess labor off the market."[11] Greenberg's interpretation of Rusche and Kirchheimer does not explain why business interests would accept the needless removal from the market of a supply of "excess labor" (individuals whose continued freedom would presumably help keep wages down), but his work does support the idea that high unemployment rates will presage high incarceration rates.

Rusche and Kirchheimer's theory was also examined by Adamson (1984), who found that "with an increase in the surplus labor force, prisoners were treated more as threats, and, consequently, prison industry was deemphasized and punishments became more severe."[12] Moreover, Inverarity and McArthy found that several recent empirical studies of imprisonment trends in the United States and Western Europe confirm Rusche and Kirchheimer's thesis that unemployment affects imprisonment directly when crime is held constant, although other factors were also significant.[13] The researchers concluded, "Our results confirm a variety of previous investigations that link rates of unemployment directly to prison admissions."[14]

More recently, Chiricos and DeLone (1992) conducted an extensive review of the issue, in which the results from forty-four empirical studies were systematically assessed. The evidence suggested that, independent of the effects of crime, labor surplus is consistently and significantly related to prison population and prison admissions. Moreover, the forty-four studies that they reviewed produced a total of 262 estimates of the relationship between labor surplus and punishment.[15] Chiricos and DeLone also concluded that the consistency and significance of the relationship of labor surplus to punishment is remarkably strong, and clearly, the state's punitive apparatus plays a direct and significant role in the control of surplus labor.[16] However, much of the data relied on by Chiricos and DeLone was very dated, and more recent data raises serious questions about their conclusions.

Other Marxist Researchers

Two other books that appeared in the 1970s were said to provide Marxist accounts of the function of imprisonment in capitalist societies in the twentieth century: Richard Quinney's *Class, State and Crime: On the Theory and Practice of Criminal Justice* (1977)[17] and Andrew Scull's *Decarceration: Community Treatment and the Deviant—A Radical View* (1977).[18] There is, however, an interesting difference in the conclusions reached by these two authors.

The prediction from Quinney is that as the "crisis of capitalism" deepens, imprisonment of the surplus population will be increasingly resorted to by the state. A significant decrease in the purchasing power of average wages over the last twenty years may be the kind of crisis that Quinney suggested would lead to the rapid expansion of incarceration rates.[19]

However, Scull took a very different view, concluding that as the fiscal crisis of the capitalist state worsens, the cost of incarceration will become increasingly oppressive and states will resort to more community treatment instead of additional incarceration. Today, state budgets everywhere are being strained to the breaking point by the cost of incarceration, and the recent addition of three strikes laws may ultimately prove Scull's prediction right. In other words, both Quinney and Scull could be correct: the rapid increase in inequality may prompt the expansion of confinement facilities, the cost of these facilities may produce a crisis that leads to the need for alternative controls, and the kind of electronically monitored house arrest that has expanded rapidly in the last five years in the United States may replace incarceration for the nondangerous property offender. The cost of such programs is so minimal that their widespread use could resolve the conundrum suggested by Quinney and Scull, namely, the need for increasingly control of offenders but at decreasing costs to the taxpayer.

DURKHEIM-BLUMSTEIN PERSPECTIVE

Zimring and Hawkins argue that the Durkheim-Blumstein period of scholarly interest in this subject was limited to a handful of studies conducted between 1973 and 1986, primarily by Alfred Blumstein of Carnegie-Mellon and his various coauthors.[20] Blumstein called his work "an important extension and significant modification of the perceptions of Durkheim"[21] although others would question Blumstein's claimed connection to Durkheim and suggest that instead his work "derived from no obvious precursors in empirical criminological scholarship or social theory."[22] Blumstein and colleagues linked their "hypothesis of the stability of punishment" to Emile Durkheim's writings on crime and punishment.[23]

Durkheim's theories on deviant behavior and the societal response to deviance included a number of different themes. At one point he argued that punishment served an independent function in bonding individuals together in their condemnation of deviance, and thereby strengthened social bonds. It is possible, therefore, that Durkheim might view the current explosion of imprisonment in the United States as an attempt to strengthen social bonds that appear to be under severe assault from the frenetic pace of social change.

From another perspective, Durkheim believed that increasing levels of punishment was a rational and predictable outcome of increasing deviance. It was this latter perspective that Blumstein claimed he was expanding and "significantly modifying" to explain varying levels of incarceration between different societies and over different periods of time.

Blumstein relies on Durkheim's discussion of penal sanctions, which was first set forth in his essay, "The Evolution of Punishment" (1900). Durkheim wrote that "the penal system was ultimately a function of the moral beliefs of society,"[24] and summed up the relationship between punishment and crime in these words: "Since punishment results from crime and expresses the manner in which it affects the public conscience, it is in the evolution of crime that one must seek the cause determining the evolution of punishment."[25] It is this relationship between crime and punishment levels with which Blumstein begins.

Blumstein, of course, was not the only theorist to make this assumption. The idea that incarceration levels are an outgrowth of crime levels has been suggested by all "social control" criminologists. These theorists take the position that any increase in incarceration in a nation is generally the natural response to an increase in the rate of crime.

However, Blumstein et al. seem to be the only researchers to have conducted an in-depth analysis of this assumption. Blumstein's thinking on this subject went through an interesting evolution, and ultimately he acknowledged that his conclusion about the stability of punishment levels was incorrect. Nonetheless, it is worth briefly reviewing his earlier findings, if only because the literature in this area is so limited.

Blumstein initially believed that there was a homeostatic, or self-regulating, punishment process. For instance, in 1973, Blumstein and Cohen concluded, "In a given society during a relatively stable period, there is a balance of forces that maintains [the rate of punishment] fairly constant."[26] In other words, when crime rates are stable, the rate of incarceration will remain stable as well. In later research, however, Blumstein and Cohen fine-tuned their theory by suggesting that it might be even when the level of crime changes, in some cases the level of punishment and the imprisonment rate per capita may remain stable.[27]

In 1979, Blumstein and Moitra studied forty-seven states between 1926 and 1974. They found "that almost half were trendless, i.e., stationary, and that the trends in the remainder were small, i.e., less than 2 percent of the mean years in all cases." The authors concluded that these findings were consistent with the general homeostatic process in that the phenomenon "appears to hold reasonably well across a wide variety of independent, albeit related, jurisdictions."[28] However, Blumstein would later question the conclusions in this study,[29] and by 1995, would reject his earlier conclusion that the rate of incarceration in a society tends to remain stable.[30]

Of course, the idea that crime rates determine incarceration rates is widely believed. Conflict theorists like Box and Hale also accept the view that an increase in prison populations is an expected result of increasing crime. They argue that the important role that the preservation of order plays in the accumulation of capital may simply be an unintended consequence of the intentional efforts of government officials to reduce crime and disorder. They concede that increasing punishment serves to shore up class domination in times when power relations are potentially threatened, but they reject the suggestion that there exists a conspiracy between state managers and capitalists to protect power relations. Rather, the preservation of class domination is viewed by Box and Hale as an unintended consequence produced by an aggregate of persons making commonsense decisions in the face of economic and political upheaval. In other words, a dramatic increase in reported crime is naturally going to lead to an increase in incarceration.[31]

RACIAL BIAS THEORY

There has been a good deal of research into the role of racism in the criminal justice system, especially in the sentencing of convicted offenders. The rate of incarceration of black males in the United States in 1991 was

3,370 per 100,000, compared to 681 per 100,000 in South Africa.[32] In other words, all other things being equal, a black South African who migrates to the United States increases his chances of winding up behind bars by fivefold. Were he to move to California, it might even be higher. One recent study showed that of all the black males in their twenties who are currently living in California, those who are either in prison, jail, on probation or on parole constitute 40 percent of the total.[33] In other words, for every 100,000 African-American males in their twenties in the state of California, 40,000 are under the control of the criminal justice system. Michael Tonry recently summarized the research in this area in his work, *Malign Neglect*. After reviewing the extensive efforts to explain the role of racism in criminal sentencing, Tonry concludes that "the evidence seems clear that the main reason that black incarceration rates are substantially higher than those for whites is that black crime rates for imprisonable crimes are substantially higher than those for whites."[34]

However, even allowing for the higher rates among African-Americans of crimes for which prison sentences are likely to be given, Tonry concludes that there still is strong evidence of racial bias influencing the growth of prisons. His analysis of the data suggests that the African-American proportion of the prison population that one should expect in a completely unbiased system of justice is around 40 percent. Why then is the present prison population in the United States actually over 50 percent black? Tonry's answer is racial prejudice. The war on drugs has resulted in a changing complexion in the prison population. The percentage of inmates who are African-American has grown rapidly and dramatically since the war on drugs began. And the political leaders who declared that war had to have known that the results would be what they have been. Tonry argues that, unlike their white counterparts, the patterns of operation employed by ghetto drug dealers make them very vulnerable to street sweeps by narcotics officers. When police are pressured by political forces to show some drug arrests, the urban street corner is where they are most likely to look for suspects. The result is that blacks are far more likely to be arrested for drugs than are whites.

Consider the numbers found by the Sentencing Project. Of all drug users in the United States, 13 percent are black. However, blacks make up 35 percent of all arrests, 55 percent of all convictions, and 74 percent of all prison sentences for drugs.

Clearly, the war on drugs has adversely, and disproportionately, impacted on African-Americans. However, since drug offenders presently account for less than one-fourth of the total prison population, we cannot explain the quadrupling of the rate of imprisonment as an outgrowth of drug policy alone.

EVALUATION OF THE LITERATURE

An examination of the current available data on incarceration levels seriously challenges the Rusche-Kirchheimer theory, the Durkheim-Blumstein theory and the Tonry race theory. Simply stated, the changes in reported crime rates, rates of unemployment and drug policies all offer necessary, but insufficient, explanations of the expansion of the prison population.

For instance, the Rusche-Kirchheimer theory was generally supported by the work of Dario Melosi, but even he acknowledged that the numbers involved suggest that imprisonment plays a symbolic rather than a functional role in regulating labor, since the number of inmates are such a small fraction of workers. Likewise, the work of Chiricos and DeLone is exhaustive and very persuasive in its support of Rusche-Kirchheimer, but their data is limited in some places and dated in others. Of the 44 studies, 14 come from England and Whales; 6 are limited to a single state and 18 are limited to a specific region in the United States. The 6 remaining studies did cover all fifty states, but the most recent was published in 1981 with data only through the late 1970s. It is inconceivable that the relationship of unemployment and incarceration rates on which Chiricos and DeLone reported has persisted following the massive growth of prisons in the last fifteen years.

Blumstein and his coauthors' perspective on incarceration does not hold up much better than Rusche and Kirchheimer's when we look at current figures on incarceration. In fact, other researchers have questioned both Blumstein's understanding of Durkheimian theory[35] and his interpretation of his own data.[36]

When Blumstein and Cohen originally advanced their hypothesis, the imprisonment rate in the United States and several Western nations had been remarkably stable over a long period of time. However, the changes made in the 1970s and 1980s contradict their conclusions. Blumstein was dealing with data up to around 1980, and Zimring and Hawkins say that the events of the following decade impeach the worth of Blumstein's view. Specifically, they explain that "the theory of the constancy of imprisonment . . . has been put to a serious strain in the rates of imprisonment in the 1980s."[37]

In fact, Blumstein himself acknowledged this. In 1980, he recognized that certain political decisions can significantly impact on incarceration rates, independent of crime rates. "Major changes in penological thinking and policy," he wrote, may result in an "increase in incarceration associated with that policy."[38]

Later, in talking about the "significant growth of 40 percent in the U.S. imprisonment rate from 1971 to 1978," Blumstein and colleagues suggested that "it is entirely possible that American society is becoming inherently more punitive and is moving to a new, higher level of 'stable punishment.' "[39]

By 1995 Blumstein looked at the figures and appeared to abandon his original argument. "The fifty-year period from the early 1920s to the early 1970s," he wrote,

> was characterized by an impressively stable incarceration rate averaging 110 per 100,000 of general population . . . and the 1993 incarceration rate of 351 per 100,000 was over three times the rate that had prevailed for the earlier fifty years. The nation had entered a new regime in which prison populations kept climbing as a replacement for the previous stable punishment policy.[40]

Moreover, Blumstein only used data available in 1993, and the rate of incarceration since that year has continued to increase. With the recent introduction of three strikes laws throughout the country, further increases are inevitable. No theory that presumes stable imprisonment rates can explain what is presently occurring.

In 1996, Jacobs and Helms correlated U.S. prison admissions between 1950 and 1990 with several social variables. They found that national crime rates are a weak predictor of prison admissions and that the national unemployment rate was "statistically insignificant" in predicting prison admissions; however, they also found that "out-of-wedlock births consistently explain imprisonment rates after these children reach 17–21 years of age."[41] However, Jacob and Helms used nationally aggregated figures—as did all their predecessors—and they offer no explanation of why the variation from state to state in prison expansion is so great while the rates of out-of-wedlock births do not vary greatly. North Carolina and South Carolina, for example, have extraordinary differences in the rate at which the imprisonment rate has changed over the past twenty years, but the rate of out-of-wedlock births in each state is virtually identical. How would Jacobs and Helms account for these figures?

In Chapter 3 and 4 we shall examine the results of correlational analysis dealing with the association between imprisonment growth and crime, as well as imprisonment growth and other social variables.

NOTES

1. Franklin E. Zimring and Gordon Hawkins, *The Scale of Imprisonment* (Chicago: University of Chicago Press, 1991), p. 14.

2. Richard A. Berk, David Rauma, Sheldon L. Messinger, and Thomas F. Cooley, "A Test of the Stability of Punishment Hypothesis: The Case of California, 1851–1970," *American Sociological Review* 46 (1981): 826.

3. Wayne N. Welsh, "Jail Overcrowding and Court Ordered Reform," in Roslyn Muraskin and Albert R. Roberts, eds., *Visions for Change: Crime and Justice in the Twenty-First Century* (Upper Saddle River, N.J.: Prentice-Hall, 1996), p. 202.

4. Paul Q. Hirst, "Marx and Engels on Law, Crime and Morality," *Economy and Society* 1 (1972): 29.

5. Peter N. Grabosky, "The Variability of Punishment," in Donald Black, ed., *Toward a General Theory of Social Control*, Vol. 1 (Orlando, Fla.: Academic Press, 1984), pp. 73–96.

6. John Braithwaite, "The Political Economy of Punishment," in E. L. Wheelwright and Ken Buckley, eds., *Essays in the Political Economy of Australian Capitalism*, Vol. 4 (Sydney, Australia: ANZ Books, 1980), p. 192.

7. David E. Barlow, Melissa Hickman Barlow, and Theodore G. Chiricos, "Long Economic Cycles and the Criminal Justice System in the United States," *Crime, Law and Social Change: An International Journal* 19, No. 2 (March 1993): 143–168.

8. See Dario Melosi, "An Introduction: Fifty Years Later: *Punishment and Social Structure* in Comparative Analysis," *Contemporary Crisis* 13 (1989): 311–326; T. G. Chiricos, "Rates of Crime and Unemployment: An Analysis of Aggregate Research Evidence," *Social Problems* 34, No. 2 (April 1987): 187–212; T. G. Chiricos and W. D. Bales, "Unemployment and Punishment: An Empirical Assessment," *Criminology* 29, No. 4 (1991): 701–715; T. G. Chiricos and M. DeLone, "Labor Surplus and Punishment: A Review and Assessment of Theory and Evidence," *Social Problems* 39, No. 4 (1992) 421–433; J. Inverarity and D. McArthy, "Punishment and Social Structure Revisited: Unemployment and Imprisonment in the United States, 1948–1984," *Sociological Quarterly* 29 (1988): 263–279.

9. Dario Melosi, "Georg Rusche and Otto Kirchheimer: *Punishment and Social Structure*," *Crime and Social Justice* 9 (1978): 79.

10. D. F. Greenberg, "The Dynamics of Oscillatory Punishment Processes," *Journal of Criminal Law and Criminology* 68 (1977): 643.

11. Ibid., p. 648.

12. C. R. Adamson, "Toward a Marxian Penology: Captive Criminal Populations as Economic Threats and Resources," *Social Problems* 31, No. 4 (1984): 436.

13. J. Inverarity and D. McArthy, "Punishment and Social Structure Revisited: Unemployment and Imprisonment in the United States, 1948–1984," *Sociological Quarterly* 29 (1988): 263.

14. Ibid., p. 279.

15. Chiricos and DeLone, "Labor Surplus and Punishment," p. 431.

16. Ibid., p. 432.

17. Richard Quinney, *Class, State and Crime: On the Theory and Practice of Criminal Justice* (New York: David McKay, 1977).

18. Andrew T. Scull, *Decarceration: Community Treatment and the Deviant—A Radical View* (Englewood Cliffs, N.J.: Prentice-Hall, 1977).

19. On this decrease, see Bennett Harrison and Barry Bluestone, *The Great U-Turn* (New York: Basic Books, 1988), p. xi; Kevin Phillips, *The Politics of Rich and Poor* (New York: Random House, 1990); Frances Fox Piven and Richard Cloward, *Regulating The Poor* (New York: Vintage Books, 1993).

20. Alfred Blumstein and Jacqueline Cohen, "A Theory of the Stability of Punishment," *Journal of Criminal Law and Criminology* 64 (1973): 198–207; Alfred Blumstein, J. Cohen, and D. Nagin, *Deterrence and Incapacitation: Estimating the Effects of Criminal Sanctions on Crime Rates* (Washington, D.C.: National Academy of Sciences, 1978), pp. 42–44; Alfred Blumstein and Soumyo Moitra, "An

Analysis of Time Series of the Imprisonment Rate in the States of the United States: A Further Test of the Stability of Punishment Hypothesis," *Journal of Criminal Law and Criminology* 70 (1979): 376–390.

21. Blumstein and Cohen, "A Theory of the Stability of Punishment," p. 207.

22. Zimring and Hawkins, *The Scale of Imprisonment*, p. 14.

23. Emile Durkheim, "The Evolution of Punishment," 1900. Rpt. in S. Lukes and A. Scull, eds., *Durkheim and the Law* (New York: St. Martin's Press, 1983), p. 121.

24. Quoted in Stephen Lukes, *Emile Durkheim: His Life and Work* (New York: Harper and Row, 1972), p. 262.

25. Durkheim, "The Evolution of Punishment."

26. Blumstein and Cohen, "A Theory of the Stability of Punishment," p. 200.

27. Blumstein and Moitra, "Analysis," p. 376.

28. Ibid., p. 390.

29. Alfred Blumstein, Jacqueline Cohen, Daniel Nagin, and Soumyo Moitra, "On Testing the Stability of Punishment Hypothesis: A Reply," *Journal of Criminal Law and Criminology* 72, No. 4 (1981): 1799–1808.

30. Alfred Blumstein, "Prisons," in James Q. Wilson and Joan Petersilia, eds., *Crime* (San Francisco: ICS Press, 1995), p. 388.

31. Steven Box and Chris Hale, "Unemployment, Imprisonment and Prison Overcrowding," *Contemporary Crisis* 9 (1985): 209–228.

32. Fox Butterfield, "U.S. Expands Its Lead in Rate of Imprisonment," *New York Times*, February 11, 1992, p. 16.

33. Fox Butterfield, "Study Examines Race and Justice in California," *New York Times*, February 13, 1996, p. A12.

34. Michael Tonry, *Malign Neglect* (New York: Oxford University Press, 1995), p. 79.

35. Greenberg, "The Dynamics of Oscillatory Punishment Processes," p. 644.

36. David Rauma, "A Concluding Note on the Stability of Punishment: Reply to Blumstein, Cohen, Moitra, and Nagin," *Journal of Criminal Law and Criminology* 72, No. 4 (1981): 1809–1812.

37. Zimring and Hawkins, *The Scale of Imprisonment*, p. 152.

38. Blumstein and Moitra, "Analysis," p. 92.

39. Blumstein et al., "On Testing the Stability of Punishment Hypothesis," pp. 1807–1809.

40. Blumstein, "Prisons," p. 388.

41. David Jacobs and Ronald D. Helms, "Toward a Political Model of Incarceration: A Time-Series Examination of Multiple Explanations for Prison Admissions Rates," *American Journal of Sociology* 102, No. 2 (September 1996): 323–355.

3

The Unusual Relationship between Crime and Imprisonment: Are Crime Rates Salient for Imprisonment Increases?

IMPRISONMENT RATES AND CRIME RATES: ARE THEY ASSOCIATED?

The fifty American states use imprisonment in very different ways. Indeed, the ratio of the variation of imprisonment rates among the fifty states is about 7½ to 1. In 1992, the range went from a high of 486 inmates per 100,000 population, in South Carolina, to a low of 67 per 100,000 population, in North Dakota (see Table 3.1). As Zimring and Hawkins phrased it:

There is in fact more diversity in rates of imprisonment among the cross section of American states than one finds when a comparison is drawn across the whole of Western Europe. The countries in Europe with the greatest diversity provide less contrast than the ten to one ratio noted in the U.S.[1]

As with their rate of imprisonment, the fifty states also show a marked variation in their rate of reported crime. In fact, the extent of the difference in crime rates among the states is more than three to one. According to the FBI's *Uniform Crime Reports*, the state with the highest rate of reported crime in 1992 was Florida, with 8,358 offenses per 100,000 population. The lowest rate of reported crime that year was in the state of West Virginia, which had just 2,609 offenses per 100,000 (see Table 3.1).

Many analysts intuitively associate the variation in crime rates with the variation in imprisonment rates. For example, in comparing Florida's imprisonment rate of 355 to West Virginia's rate of just 92, the intuitive assumption that there is a relationship between crime and imprisonment

Table 3.1
Imprisonment Rate, Crime Rate in 1992 and Imprisonment Rate Increases for All
Fifty States

	imprisonment rate		UCR rate	imprisonment % increase
1. SC	486		5,893	30
2. LA	484		6,546	423
3. OK	459		5,431	228
4. NV	448		6,203	270
5. MI	413		5,610	340
6. AZ	409		7,020	430
7. AL	407		5,268	294
8. DE	390		4,848	690
9. MD	381		6,224	175
10.GA	365		6,405	110
11.FL	355		8,358	155
12.OH	347		4,665	350
13.TX	344		7,057	153
14.NY	340		5,858	430
15.AR	340		4,761	325
16.CA	339		6,671	305
17.MS	327		4,282	295
18.VA	327		4,298	207
19.AL	327		5,569	435
20.MO	311		5,097	320
21.NC	290		5,802	82
22.NJ	290		5,064	301
23.KY	274		3,223	210
24.IL	271		5,765	435
25.CT	268		4,848	439
26.CO	256		5,958	215
27.IN	242		4,686	235
28.KS	238		5,319	225
29.TN	234		5,135	185
30.WY	226		4,575	200
31.ID	209		3,996	320
32.SD	208		2,998	305
33.PA	207		3,392	293
34.NM	197		6,434	253
35.WA	192		6,172	150
36.MT	180		4,596	355
37.WI	176		4,319	290
38.OR	174		5,820	105
39.RI	170		4,578	370
40.HI	164		6,112	325
41.MA	161		5,002	200
42.NH	160		3,080	420
43.IA	160		3,957	251
44.NE	151		4,324	140
45.VT	151		3,410	401
46.UT	146		5,658	185
47.ME	121		3,523	162
48.WV	92		2,609	55
49.MN	85		4,590	150
50.ND	67		2,903	130

Source: Adapted by Joseph Dillon Davey from U.S. Department of Justice, *Sourcebook of Criminal Justice Statistics, 1993* (Washington, D.C.: Bureau of Justice Statistics, 1994).

would seem to be supported. However, this relationship is clearly lacking in other areas of the nation.

Recall, for instance, the unusual case of the Dakotas. South Dakota and North Dakota have very similar rates of crime, but the rate of imprisonment in the two states became very different after 1972, when the rate of imprisonment in the two states was close. Between 1972 and 1992, South Dakota increased its imprisonment rate over 300 percent, and today, its rate of imprisonment is more than triple that of North Dakota and the crime rate remains virtually identical. Is it the crime level in a state that determines the imprisonment rate? Does the experience in the Dakotas hold up in a fifty-state data set for the twenty years between 1972 and 1992?

The relationship between crime rates and imprisonment rates also disappears when we compare states like Ohio and New Mexico. Ohio's crime rate (4,665) is far lower than New Mexico's (6,434), but its imprisonment rate (347) is almost double (197). Utah, on the other hand, has a much higher crime rate (5,658) than Virginia (4,298), but less than half the rate of imprisonment (146 versus 327).

In other words, states with high crime rates sometimes also have high rates of imprisonment, but sometimes they do not. While examples of confluence between crime and imprisonment rates can be found in the data, glaring exceptions to this rule are also apparent throughout. Do states with high rates of crime generally have high rates of imprisonment, or is the relationship capricious?

Earlier Research

Until recently the assumption that the imprisonment rate in a given state was associated with the crime rate in that state was intuitively assumed but rarely tested. The problem with both official and unofficial crime statistics is well known.[2] Research data on imprisonment was at a very primitive level prior to the surge in the crime rate in the 1960s and the enormous accompanying surge in federal spending on criminal justice research. Even such commonplace information like the number of prisons that were operated in the United States was difficult to find prior to the 1960s.

As a result, attempts to correlate levels of crime and imprisonment nationwide have been very rare. Many studies were limited to a single state, a small group of states or, sometimes, different regions of the country. Among most commentators the implicit assumption on the subject of crime and prisons was the commonsense view that prison populations in a given state are a reflection of that state's crime level.

However, Zimring and Hawkins (1991) studied the relationship between crime and imprisonment nationwide and concluded: "It seems clear that levels of imprisonment in the U.S. vary widely both over time and from state to state. It is evident also that these variations are largely independent of variations in either crime rates or the provisions of penal codes."[3]

Table 3.1 shows the data necessary to conduct a bivariate correlation between the 1992 imprisonment rate and the 1992 UCR rate for each of the fifty states. As is shown in Appendix 5, that comparison yielded a reasonably strong correlation coefficient (.5678), which has gotten much stronger since 1972; however, the correlation still leaves a good deal to be explained. The amount of reported crime in a given state is far from perfect as a predictor of the level of imprisonment in that state. Therefore, other factors must be at work. For example, a state's imprisonment rate is also strongly related to the percentage of blacks.

Numerous researchers have made the argument that incarceration rates seem to reflect differences in the laws and legal cultures of different areas and the harshness of local policies regarding punishment.[4] Thus, perhaps it should not be surprising that high crime rates are not a foolproof predictor of high imprisonment rates. However, what of the more central question asked here, namely, whether changes in rates of crime predict changes in the rate of imprisonment. If the crime rate increases in a given state, will that predict an increase in the imprisonment level?

CHANGES IN IMPRISONMENT RATES AND CRIME RATES: ARE THEY ASSOCIATED?

My interest is not in explaining differences among the states in incarceration rates but in looking at the variation among the fifty states in the increase in those rates. We saw that the variation between the highest and lowest crime rates is a little over three to one, but what about the variation in the changes in crime rates?

The data indicate that the rate of reported crime increased in every state during the 1972–1992 period, but once again, the rate of increase varied widely. While the average increase in the rate of reported crime in each state for this period was 49 percent, the increase varied from a low of 4 percent in Michigan to a high of 137 percent in Mississippi (see Table 3.2).

How do these crime rate increases compare with the increases in imprisonment rates? The increases in imprisonment rate in these two states were slightly above the national average: Mississippi increased by 295 percent and Michigan, by 340 percent. Thus, while the ratio of crime rate increase between Michigan and Mississippi is 34 to 1 (134 to 4 percent), the differences in the rate at which the states increased their imprisonment rates is minuscule (and in opposite directions).

The ratio of the variation among the fifty states in the increase in imprisonment rate between 1972 and 1992 is close to 13 to 1, with Delaware and West Virginia at the extremes. What happened in these states to explain such divergent increases?

Table 3.2
Increase in Imprisonment Rates and Crime Rates, 1972–1992, for All Fifty States

percentage increase in:

		imprisonment	U.C.R.
1.	DE	690%	7%
2.	AK	435	24
3.	IL	435	52
4.	AZ	430	18
5.	NY	430	38
6.	LA	423	93
7.	NH	420	54
8.	VT	401	54
9.	MA	400	21
10.	RI	370	5
11.	MT	355	43
12.	OH	350	35
13.	CT	349	42
14.	MI	340	4
15.	HI	325	32
16.	AR	325	119
17.	ID	320	16
18.	MO	320	29
19.	SD	305	40
20.	CA	305	5
21.	NJ	301	31
22.	SC	300	80
23.	MS	295	137
24.	AL	294	126
25.	PA	293	43
26.	WI	290	46
27.	NV	270	6
28.	NM	253	36
29.	IA	251	56
30.	IN	235	45
31.	OK	228	74
32.	KS	225	56
33.	CO	215	6
34.	KY	210	44
35.	VA	207	39
36.	WY	200	48
37.	TN	185	94
38.	UT	185	34
39.	MD	175	34
40.	ME	162	51
41.	TX	153	83
42.	FL	155	55
43.	MN	150	29
44.	WA	150	31
45.	NE	140	64
46.	ND	130	46
47.	GA	110	109
48.	OR	105	15
49.	NC	82	118
50.	WV	55	81

Source: Adapted by Joseph Dillon Davey from U.S. Department of Justice, *Sourcebook of Criminal Justice Statistics, 1993* (Washington, D.C.: Bureau of Justice Statistics, 1994).

It is commonly assumed that the sequence leading to prison overcrowding begins with an increase in the "crime rate." The increase in the
rate of reported crime is presumed to result in increases in felony convictions and prison sentences. This sequence, however, is not apparent in the
crime and prison statistics for the two decades following 1972.

The data indicate that every state showed an increase in incarceration
rate between 1972 and 1992. The average increase was around 250 percent
(from 93 to 330 per 100,000 population nationwide). However, the range
of variation in increases in incarceration rates extended from 55 percent,
in West Virginia, to 690 percent, in Delaware. Moreover, the variation is
not limited to a few extremes on each end (see Table 3.2).

Zimring and Hawkins used national aggregate statistics to examine the
correlation between crime increases and imprisonment increases. When
they found little association between national crime rates and national rates
of imprisonment, they limited their measurements to only violent crime,
which is most likely to result in a prison term. Again, however, the association proved weak.

Zimring and Hawkins then experimented with different lag times on the
grounds that if crime increased, it might be a year or two before it would
be reflected in an imprisonment increase. They found that "the correlation
between the degree of increase in index crime in one year during the period
and changes in the rates of imprisonment during the next calendar year is
in fact negative: $-.29$."[5] In other words, one or more factors other than
changes in the crime rate were influencing the growth of imprisonment.

Since the work of Zimring and Hawkins, other researchers have studied
the relationship between crime increases and the imprisonment increases
that lead to overcrowded conditions. Their conclusions have generally been
that "there is little support for the crime-causes-overcrowding hypothesis."[6]
In 1995, a study by Alfred Blumstein concluded that the crimes of murder,
robbery and burglary "did not increase dramatically between the 1970s
and the mid-1990s, thereby making it very unlikely that the growth in
prison population was a consequence of growing crime rates."[7] Clearly,
Zimring and Hawkins have some support for their conclusions.

However, it is possible that Zimring and Hawkins missed something by
using national figures in their analysis of the relationship between crime
and imprisonment rates. Could it be that by aggregating the crime and
imprisonment rate data on a national level, as they did, or by relying on
specific examples, Zimring and Hawkins had concealed a significant relationship?

In the part of their study where Zimring and Hawkins relied on national
data, they risk overaggregating by relying on mean averages, which can
present an extremely deceptive picture. In theory, their aggregate analysis
could hide polar differences between some states with rapid growth of both
crime and imprisonment and others with none.

In other words, if a comparison was made of changes in national crime rates and national imprisonment rates and no association was apparent, could it be that there is actually a hidden association between crime and imprisonment? For instance, assume that the national crime rate does not change in a given year but the imprisonment rate goes up. Nationally aggregated figures would suggest no association between the two, which is what Zimring and Hawkins found.

However, it is possible that some states may have had a substantial increase in crime and a very high increase in the rate of imprisonment while others had a substantial decrease in crime and no change in imprisonment rate. In the aggregate, then, we would expect to see a stable crime rate and a climbing imprisonment rate, and hence, no association between the two. Such figures would thus hide the association between crime and imprisonment rates.

It is possible that this hidden association could be made apparent by taking the twenty-five states with the highest increases and comparing them to the twenty-five states with the lowest increases. Consider Tables 3.3 and 3.4. Do the high-increase states, which invested in more prisons, show less increase in crime than the low-increase states over the twenty years between 1972 and 1992? Since the National Crime Survey does not disaggregate data on a state level, a comparison of each state's "reported" crime according to the Uniform Crime Reports must be relied on. A comparison of the twenty-five states with high increases in imprisonment with the remaining twenty-five states shows that the twenty-year increase in reported crime was slightly higher in the states that had low increases in imprisonment.

If the data were disaggregated into a fifty-state data set over the twenty year period, would the association between increases in crime rate and increases in imprisonment rate (seen in Tables 3.3 and 3.4) continue to hold? In other words, is there a correlation between the level of crime rate increase in each of the fifty states and the corresponding increase in the level of imprisonment? If so, it will be apparent in a bivariate correlation between the two variables in the fifty states.

Table 3.2 contains the data for a bivariate correlation of the imprisonment increase and the changes in reported crime for each of the fifty states, which should reveal whether there is, in fact, an association between the two. However, as can be seen in Appendix 5, the correlation between the increase in reported crime (CRIMINCP) and the increase in imprisonment for the fifty states over twenty years (PRISINCP) actually has a correlational coefficient of $-.2685, p = .059$. In short, a rising crime rate evidently has a negative impact on the growth of incarceration.

This result is so counterintuitive that it seems worth further analysis. As can be seen in Appendix 5, a multiple regression analysis of the increase in the crime rate (CRIMINC) and the increase in the imprisonment rate (PRISINCP) is consistent with the bivariate correlation. Since the standard error

Table 3.3

The Twenty-Five States with the Highest Imprisonment Rate Increases between 1972 and 1992

		% INCREASE IN IMPRISONMENT	UCR
1.	DE	690	7
2.	AK	435	24
3.	IL	435	52
4.	AZ	430	18
5.	NY	430	38
6.	LA	423	93
7.	NH	420	54
8.	VT	401	54
9.	MA	400	21
10.	RI	370	5
11.	MT	355	43
12.	OH	350	35
13.	CT	349	42
14.	MI	340	4
15.	HI	325	32
16.	AR	325	119
17.	ID	320	16
18.	MO	320	29
19.	SD	305	40
20.	CA	305	5
21.	NJ	301	31
22.	SC	300	80
23.	MS	295	137
24.	AL	294	126
25.	PA	293	43
	AVERAGE INCREASE	368%	46%

Source: Adapted by Joseph Dillon Davey from U.S. Department of Justice, *Sourcebook of Criminal Justice Statistics, 1993* (Washington, D.C.: Bureau of Justice Statistics, 1994).

of the beta of CRIMINC is actually higher than the beta, we can conclude that it is a very poor predictor of PRISINCP.

This association between imprisonment increases and crime increases is close to the figure of $-.29$ found by Zimring and Hawkins in their analysis of lagged national data. Clearly, rising crime rates are an inadequate predictor of rising imprisonment rates. Something else was the driving force in the imprisonment increases from 1972 to 1992.

Could this driving force have been an increase in homicide rates? Homicide is both the most accurately counted of all felonies (it is estimated that over 98 percent of homicides are reported) and the crime most likely to result in imprisonment. Homicide rates vary widely among the states, from a high of 20.3 per 100,000 population, in Louisiana, to a low of 1.6 per 100,000, in Maine. Is there an association between high homicide rates and high increases in imprisonment rates?

Table 3.5 shows the average homicide rate for 1993 in the twenty-five states with the highest increases in imprisonment, and Table 3.6 shows the

Table 3.4

The Twenty-Five States with the Lowest Imprisonment Rate Increases between 1972 and 1992

	% INCREASE IN INCARCERATION	UCR
26. WI	290	46
27. NV	270	6
28. NM	253	36
29. IA	251	56
30. IN	235	45
31. OK	228	74
32. KS	225	56
33. CO	215	6
34. KY	210	44
35. VA	207	39
36. WY	200	48
37. TN	185	94
38. UT	185	34
39. MD	175	34
40. ME	162	51
41. TX	153	83
42. FL	155	55
43. MN	150	29
44. WA	150	31
45. NE	140	64
46. ND	130	46
47. GA	110	109
48. OR	105	15
49. NC	82	118
50. WV	55	81
AVERAGE INCREASE	181%	52%

Source: Adapted by Joseph Dillon Davey from U.S. Department of Justice, Sourcebook of Criminal Justice Statistics, 1993 (Washington, D.C.: Bureau of Justice Statistics, 1994).

same figure for the twenty-five states with the lowest rates of increase. The rate for the low-increase states is almost 20 percent lower than the rate for the high-increase states. Could the increase in imprisonment be connected to changes in the homicide rate? Probably it is not. First of all, despite a quadrupling of the imprisonment rate, the rate of homicide nationwide did not change very much between 1972 and 1992, remaining at a little over 9 per 100,000 population for both years. The rate peaked in 1980 at 10.2 per 100,000, whereas the biggest imprisonment increases started around 1984. Second, the UCR shows 1,500 serious offenses for every homicide, and homicide only accounts for a small proportion of all prison admissions. In 1993, for instance, of all those admitted to state prisons, just 3.5 percent had been sentenced for homicide.[8] These numbers strongly suggest that variations in homicide rates cannot explain variations in imprisonment rates. Chapter 4 describes a correlational analysis of imprisonment rate increases and homicide rates that further supports this conclusion.

Table 3.5
Increases in Imprisonment, Crime Rate, Homicide Rate and Rate of Drug Arrests:
High-Increase States

		% INCREASE IN Imprisonment	UCR	hom rate	drug arrests
1.	DE	690	7	5.0	334
2.	ALASKA	435	24	9.0	101
3.	IL	435	52	7.4	101
4.	AZ	430	18	8.6	383
5.	NY	430	38	13.3	683
6.	LA	423	93	20.3	309
7.	NH	420	54	2.0	162
8.	VT	401	54	3.6	86
9.	MA	400	21	3.9	254
10.	RI	370	5	3.9	281
11.	MT	355	43	3.0	129
12.	OH	350	35	6.0	91
13.	CT	349	42	6.3	571
14.	MI	340	4	9.8	297
15.	HI	325	32	3.6	325
16.	ARK	325	119	10.2	256
17.	ID	320	16	2.9	175
18.	MO	320	29	11.3	269
19.	SD	305	40	3.4	61
20.	CA	305	5	13.1	839
21.	NJ	301	31	5.3	600
22.	SC	300	80	10.3	430
23.	MS	295	137	13.5	178
24.	AL	294	126	11.6	188
25.	PA	293	43	6.8	233
	AVERAGE INCREASE	368%	46%	7.8	293

Source: Adapted by Joseph Dillon Davey from U.S. Department of Justice, *Sourcebook of Criminal Justice Statistics, 1993* (Washington, D.C.: Bureau of Justice Statistics, 1994).

CONCLUSION

The correlation coefficient between increases in imprisonment and increases in crime is $-.2685$, $p = .059$; it would, therefore, be unreasonable to explain a state's prison expansion simply as a reaction to the crime problem. This point was made by a study done for the U.S. Department of Justice in 1991. Robyn Cohen of the Bureau of Justice Statistics studied the recent imprisonment increases per reported crime and concluded that

in 1970, only 23 people were incarcerated for every 1,000 reported index crimes. Commitment probability increased steadily throughout the 1980s, reaching 43 per 1,000 crimes by 1990, an increase of 72 percent between 1980 and 1990. Similarly, while 196 of every 1,000 adults arrested for serious crimes were incarcerated in 1980, the rate rose to 392 per 1,000 by 1990.[9]

In other words, crime rates per 1,000 population were not increasing, yet imprisonment rates per 1,000 crimes were increasing.[10] Moreover, state

Table 3.6
Increases in Imprisonment, Crime Rate, Homicide Rate and Rate of Drug Arrests:
Low-Increase States

	% INCREASE IN Imprisonment	UCR	hom rate	drug arrests
26. WI	290	46	4.4	192
27. NV	270	6	10.4	560
28. NM	253	36	8.0	220
29. IA	251	56	2.3	116
30. IN	235	45	7.5	110
31. OK	228	74	8.4	284
32. KS	225	56	6.4	223
33. CO	215	6	5.8	228
34. KY	210	44	6.6	315
35. VA	207	39	8.3	285
36. WY	200	48	3.4	121
37. TN	185	94	10.2	241
38. UT	185	34	3.1	190
39. MD	175	34	12.7	599
40. ME	162	51	1.6	187
41. FL	155	55	8.9	506
42. TX	153	83	11.9	366
43. MN	150	29	3.4	126
44. WA	150	31	5.2	220
45. NE	140	64	3.9	253
46. ND	130	46	1.7	66
47. GA	110	109	11.4	272
48. OR	105	15	4.6	346
49. NC	82	118	11.3	376
50. WV	55	81	6.9	88
AVERAGE INCREASE	181%	52%	6.2	259

Source: Adapted by Joseph Dillon Davey from U.S. Department of Justice, *Sourcebook of Criminal Justice Statistics, 1993* (Washington, D.C.: Bureau of Justice Statistics, 1994).

variations argue that this was an outgrowth of policy decisions made in each of the fifty states. What social variables in each of the states are associated with their differing punishment policies? Chapter 4 considers some of the "usual suspects."

NOTES

1. Franklin E. Zimring and Gordon Hawkins, *The Scale of Imprisonment* (Chicago: University of Chicago Press, 1991), p. 150.

2. Wesley G. Skogan, "Measurement Problems in Official and Survey Crime Rates," *Journal of Criminal Justice* 3 (1975): 17–32.

3. Zimring and Hawkins, *The Scale of Imprisonment*, p. 220.

4. See, for example, Carol A. Kizziah, *The State of the Jails in California. Report No. 1: Overcrowding in the Jails* (Sacramento, Calif.: Board of Corrections, State of California, 1984); John Klofas, "The Jail and the Community," *Justice Quarterly* 7 (1990): 69–104; Wayne N. Welsh, Henry N. Pontell, Mathew C. Le-

one, and Patrick Kinkade, "Jail Overcrowding: An Analysis of Policy Makers' Perceptions," *Justice Quarterly* 7 (1990): 341–370.

5. Zimring and Hawkins, *The Scale of Imprisonment*, p. 122.

6. Wayne N. Welsh, "Jail Overcrowding and Court Ordered Reform," in Roslyn Muraskin and Albert R. Roberts, eds., *Visions for Change: Crime and Justice in the Twenty-First Century* (Upper Saddle River, N.J.: Prentice-Hall, 1996), p. 201.

7. Alfred Blumstein, "Prisons," in James Q. Wilson and Joan Petersilia, *Crime* (San Francisco: ICS Press, 1995), p. 391.

8. U.S. Department of Justice. *Sourcebook of Criminal Justice Statistics, 1994* (Washington, D.C.: Bureau of Justice Statistics 1995), p. 552.

9. Robyn Cohen, *Prisoners in 1990* (Washington, D.C.: Bureau of Justice Statistics, 1991), p. 2.

10. Concerning the crime rates, see Joseph Dillon Davey, "Crime in America Is Less Than You Think," *Human Rights* 21, No. 2 (Spring 1994): 1.

4

Socioeconomic Variables: Are the "Usual Suspects" Salient for Imprisonment Increases?

WHAT ARE THE "USUAL SUSPECTS"?

We began with the assumption that there are essentially three leading explanations for the increase in imprisonment. The Durkheim-Blumstein thesis suggested that crime rates predict imprisonment rates. However, a bivariate correlation between the changes in the rate of crime (CRIMINCP) and the rate of imprisonment (PRISINCP) suggests that, not only is there a weak relationship between these two variables, but it is (as Zimring and Hawkins found using nationally aggregated data) a negative relationship.

In short, the figures show that the increase in the rate of imprisonment in each of the fifty states between 1972 and 1992 has a coefficient of correlation of $-.2685$, $p = .059$, with respective increases in the reported crime rate. It appears that whatever the reason for the sudden increase in imprisonment, the variable of reported crime rates in the FBI's *Uniform Crime Reports*—essentially the exclusive source of crime statistics for the media and the public—has little explanatory power. It was not an increase in crime that resulted in increased imprisonment, but an increase in the proportion of reported crimes that resulted in a sentence of imprisonment, as Robyn Cohen pointed out.

However, this increasing punitiveness was very unevenly spread among the states. As shown in Tables 3.1 through 3.6, the ratio of the highest to lowest rate of increase in the imprisonment rate between 1972 and 1992 was greater than thirteen to one, with almost as many states over the average increase as were under it. What social variables, other than crime rates, might be salient to explain the very pronounced differences in imprisonment rate increases?

As described in Chapter 1, Michael Tonry argued that the recent growth of imprisonment is an outgrowth of racist criminal justice policies. As Tonry sees it, part of the reason for the disproportionate number of black inmates is their high rate of violent crime, and another part is that blacks were the target of the war on drugs.[1] Consequently, it should be useful to ask whether there is a correlation between the rate of increase in a state's prison population, on the one hand, and the proportion of that state's inhabitants who are black, the rate of drug arrests, and the rate of homicide, on the other.[2]

An alternative to the Durkheim-Blumstein thesis and the Tonry race thesis is Rusche and Kirchheimer's Marxist perspective regarding this problem (see Chapter 1). They argued that economic factors had determined imprisonment levels and that prisons were used as a weapon in class conflict. It would therefore be useful to do a correlational analysis between imprisonment increases in the fifty states, on the one hand, and poverty, rates of unemployment, and average income, on the other.[2]

In recent years demographers have become more influential in explaining the rise and fall of crime rates. Demographers have long known that the "crime-prone age group" (14- to 24-year-olds) is disproportionately criminal. The 76 million individuals born between 1946 and 1964 are called the "baby boomers." These individuals started reaching the crime-prone age in 1960, and the predictable boom in crime rates did not surprise demographers. It might also be useful, therefore, to add a final correlational analysis comparing the proportion of youth in a state with its increase in imprisonment level. As a result, the independent variables that I correlated with the states' increases in imprisonment rates are the following.

Rusche-Kirchheimer Variables

Poverty. The average inmate in U.S. prisons is far more likely to have lived in poverty at some time in his or her life than a noninmate. Consequently, I measured the percentage of the population in each state that lived under the poverty level.

Unemployment. It is an article of faith among many researchers in the field that unemployment levels impact on imprisonment levels, so I compared the unemployment rates of each state.

Income. While Rusche and Kirchheimer did not associate relative wealth of a society with imprisonment rates, some researchers have suggested that the expense of prison is actually a luxury that only wealthy states can afford. Therefore, I compared the average per capita income of each of the sixteen states in my study.

Tonry Variables

Race. Since African-Americans make up a disproportionate number of the inmates in the nation's prisons, I measured the percentage of each state's population that was African-American.

Homicide Rate. Since homicide is both the most accurately counted of all crimes and the one most likely to result in a prison sentence, I measured the homicide rate of each state.

Drug Arrests. To what extent did the war on drugs explain the rapid increase in imprisonment?

Demographic Variable

Age. A state with an unusually young population may well be expected to have higher rates of imprisonment, I compared the percentage of the population of each state that was under eighteen years of age.

CORRELATIONAL ANALYSIS

States on Extreme Ends

If the states with the highest and the lowest changes in imprisonment rates were contrasted, would the contrast reveal an association between imprisonment changes and the suspected social variables? Table 4.1 shows the rate of change for the eight states with the greatest increase in imprisonment rates (with an average increase of 462 percent) and the eight states with the lowest increase in imprisonment rates (average increase, 110 percent). Would the suspected social variables be salient for explaining differences in rates of imprisonment change?

As can be seen from Table 4.2, there were no surprising differences in the group of states with the highest or lowest increases in imprisonment for any of the variables. The high-increase states had a 17 percent higher average income and an 11 percent lower rate of poverty, notwithstanding a 14 percent higher rate of unemployment. There were no differences in age distribution in the sixteen states, and so this variable was discarded from the fifty-state data set.

However, the states with the highest imprisonment increases do show about a 12 percent higher percentage of blacks in their population, which would tend to support Michael Tonry's thesis that the war on drugs is, in fact, a war on African-Americans.[3] Tonry argued that since police find it easier to make their quota of drug arrests in the ghettos, any policy designed to "get tough" on drugs necessarily meant that more blacks would be imprisoned. Tonry's theory would seem to be corroborated by a study done by the Sentencing Commission which found that while blacks make

Table 4.1
States with the Highest and Lowest Increases in Imprisonment Rates between
1972 and 1992 (all rates are per 100,000 population)

```
(high-increase states)
Delaware                  690%
Alaska                    535%
New York                  432%
Arizona                   430%
Louisiana                 423%
New Hampshire             420%
Vermont                   401%
Massachusetts             400%
                          -----
AVERAGE INCREASE          466%



(low-increase states)
West Virginia              55%
North Carolina             82%
Oregon                    105%
Georgia                   110%
North Dakota              130%
Nebraska                  140%
Washington                150%
Minnesota                 150%
                          -----
AVERAGE INCREASE          115%
```

Source: Adapted by Joseph Dillon Davey from U.S. Department of Justice, *Sourcebook of
   Criminal Justice Statistics, 1993* (Washington, D.C.: Bureau of Justice Statistics, 1994).

up 12 percent of the population and 13 percent of drug users, they account
for 35 percent of all drug arrests, 55 percent of all drug convictions and
74 percent of all prison sentences for drug offenses.[4]

Moreover, the rates of drug arrests also appear to be significantly different in the two sets of states. The high-increase states had an average of 289
arrests per 100,000 population, while the low increase states had just 218.
We will examine the role of the drug war on prison expansion in Chapter
6.

On the other hand, Tonry acknowledged that higher rates of violence in
the black community should be expected to result in higher rates of imprisonment in states with a high percentage of black residents. In 1993, for
instance, 51 percent of all homicide victims in the United States were
black,[5] and the correlational analysis in Appendix 5 shows a strong relationship between the black population and homicide rates (.8270 in 1972
and .7849 in 1992).

Moreover, homicide is both the offense most likely to lead to a sentence
of imprisonment and the most accurately counted of all criminal offenses.
Therefore, a comparison of homicide rates between these two sets of ex-

Table 4.2

Comparison of States with High Increases and States with Low Increases in Imprisonment Rates on Seven Social Variables

HIGH INCREASE STATES

	Percent blacks	Average income (x $1,000)	% Below pov. lev.	Rate of unemploy	%Under 18	Hom* rate	Drug* arrest
DE	16.8	15.8	8.7	5.2	24.5	5.0	334
AL	4.0	17.6	9.0	7.0	31.3	9.0	101
NY	15.9	16.5	13.0	5.2	23.7	13.3	683
AZ	0.3	13.4	15.7	5.3	25.0	8.6	383
LA	30.8	10.6	23.3	6.2	30.3	20.3	309
NH	0.7	15.9	6.4	5.7	25.1	2.0	162
VT	0.4	13.5	9.9	4.9	25.4	3.6	86
MA	4.9	17.2	8.9	6.0	22.5	3.9	254
Avg.	9.2	15.1	11.9	5.69	26.0	8.2	289

(* Both homicide rate and drug arrest rate are per 100,000 population)

LOW INCREASE STATES

	Percent blacks	Average income (x $1,000)	% Below pov. lev.	Rate of unemploy	%Under 18	Hom* rate	Drug* arrest
WV	3.1	10.5	19.7	8.3	24.7	6.9	88
NC	21.9	12.8	13.0	4.0	24.2	11.3	376
OR	1.6	13.4	12.4	5.5	25.4	4.6	346
GA	29.9	13.6	14.0	5.4	26.6	11.4	272
ND	.5	11.0	14.4	4.0	27.4	1.7	66
NE	3.6	12.4	11.1	2.1	27.1	3.9	253
WA	3.0	14.9	10.9	4.8	25.9	5.2	220
MN	2.1	14.3	10.2	4.8	26.6	3.4	126
Avg.	8.2	12.9	13.2	4.86	26.0	6.05	218

(* Both homicide rate and drug arrest rate are per 100,000 population)

Source: Adapted by Joseph Dillon Davey from Alan Carpenter and Carl Provorse, *The World Almanac of the United States* (Mahwah, N.J.: Funk and Wagnalls, 1993).

treme states might prove fruitful. While the high-increase states do show a higher rate of homicide, both sets of states have an average homicide rate below 9.3 per 100,000, the average for all states in 1992. Furthermore, of all prison admissions in the United States only about 3.5 percent are for homicide. It is unlikely, therefore, that varying homicide rates can explain the differences in imprisonment rate increases among these sixteen states.

Table 4.3
Fifty-State Data Set: Correlation between Imprisonment Rate Increases
(PRISINCP) and the "Usual Suspects" between 1972 and 1992

Variable	Correlational coefficient
1. % of population that is black (BLACK92)	.0799 p=.581
2. Homicide rate (HOM92)	.0567 p=696
3. Rate of crime (UCR92)	−.0194 p=.894
4. Increase in the homicide rate (HOMINC)	.1498 p=.299
5. Rate of imprisonment in 1972 (PRISON72)	−.3852 p=006
6. Increase in crime rate (CRIMINCP)	−.2685 p=059
7. Average per capita income (VAR 8)	.2841 p=.046
8. % population below poverty level (VAR 9)	−.1400 p=.332
9. Unemployment rate (VAR 10)	.1964 p=.172
10. Rate of drug arrests (VAR 11)	.0680 p=639

Fifty-State Data Set

Clearly, none of the variables that have been considered here (see Table
4.3) are very salient for explaining differences in imprisonment changes
when comparing the averages of the sixteen states on the extreme ends.
Still, it could be possible that a bivariate correlation of all fifty states will
show a significant association. If the changes in imprisonment rate in each
of the fifty states are correlated with each of the "usual suspects," will any
coefficients stand out? Appendixes 5 and 6 report the correlational analysis
measuring the association between the increase in the rate of imprisonment
and sixteen other variables.

Some general observations can be drawn from the data gathered here, some of which are expected, while others are difficult to understand. For instance, it is predictable that states that had a high rate of imprisonment in 1972 would see a smaller rate of increase in imprisonment rate during the next two decades. This, of course, should be expected inasmuch as a high starting base requires a greater increase to change the increase rate than would a low base. Therefore, the rate of imprisonment in 1972 (PRISON72) and the increase in the imprisonment rate (PRISINCP) show a negative association ($-.3852$). In other words, states with high rates in 1972 generally increased their rate more slowly than states with a low rate in 1972.

A surprising association exists between economic factors and drug arrests. The association between the rate of drug arrests in a state (DRUG92) and the per capita income of that state (INCPC92) is a powerful one (.5291). In other words, as the relative wealth of a state increases, so does the rate of drug arrests. Moreover, there is a negative association between drug arrests and the rate of poverty (POV92), which implies again that the poorer a state is, the lower the rate of drug arrests.

These correlations between drug arrests and wealth or poverty probably suggest that wealthy states have the resources to indulge themselves in the luxury of massive numbers of arrests for drug use, as well as greater drug consumption, while the poorer states have fewer arrests and less drug consumption. Since there are an estimated 12 million users of hard drugs, it is likely that all states have an ample supply of drug users to fill whatever drug arrest quotas they may set. The decision to set high quotas would be a political one, based, at least in part, on the resources available for incarcerating drug offenders.

Tonry's Variables. The correlational analysis shown in Appendixes A and B strongly suggest that states with high rates of crime, high rates of homicide and high rates of African-Americans are, as would be expected, also states with high rates of imprisonment. The respective correlations were .5678, between crime and imprisonment, .6097 between homicide rates and imprisonment, and .5118 between rates of African-Americans and imprisonment.

However, we should also investigate whether there is an association between a state's black population, homicide rate or rate of drug arrests and an increase in its rate of imprisonment.

The fifty American states vary in their percentage of black population, from less than 1 percent in Iowa to over 35 percent in Mississippi. The association between a large black population in the 1990 census (BLACK90P)[6] and the rate of reported crime (UCR92) is only .1806. However, the association between the black population and the rate of imprisonment (PRISON92) is significant, at .5118. In other words, states with a large percentage of blacks do not necessarily have a high rate of crime, but they do have a high rate of imprisonment.

What of changes in imprisonment rates? Did states with a higher proportion of blacks in their population experience a higher rate of imprisonment increase?

As Appendix 5 shows, the coefficient of correlation between BLACK90P and PRISINCP was just .0799, hardly a significant association. Given the increase between 1972 and 1992 in the proportion of inmates nationwide who are black, it is surprising that a high proportion of African-Americans in a state's population is not more salient for explaining imprisonment rate increases. It may be that with over 30 million African-Americans, every state has an ample pool of blacks to increase its prison population.

What about the rate of drug arrests? Did the war on drugs explain the increase in imprisonment? There is no doubt that far more drug offenders are being incarcerated today than in the past, but can we explain the variation in the rate of increase from one state to the next according to their different levels of drug arrests per capita? Even among the sixteen states on the extreme ends of imprisonment growth, the variation in drug arrests per 100,000 population is shocking. For example, New York reported more than ten times the number of drug arrests per 100,000 population than did North Dakota.

Do variations in drug arrests among the fifty states explain variations in imprisonment growth? The answer is clearly no. The correlation between the rate of drug arrests (DRUG92) and the growth of the imprisonment rate (PRISINC) is a very weak .0692. The war on drugs may be increasing the national rate of imprisonment, but it explains very little about the variation in the increases from state to state.

Do homicide rates or increases in homicide rates explain the variation in imprisonment growth? The rate of homicide in a state (HOM92) may be salient for explaining the rate of imprisonment in that state, but it is not salient for explaining changes in the state's imprisonment rate over time. The correlation between the homicide rate and the imprisonment increase was an insignificant .0567. Moreover, the correlation between the increase in homicide rates (HOMINC) and the increase in imprisonment (PRISINCP) is an insignificant .1498.

In short, there is little support for the theory that the variation in the growth in imprisonment is related to race, drug arrests, or the homicide rate, although the level of imprisonment at any given time is related to the proportion of the population that is black.

Rusche and Kirchheimer's Variables. An interesting, and somewhat expected, association is evident in the relationship between the wealth of a state and its rate of imprisonment increase. Prisons are expensive. It should not come as a surprise, then, that wealth and poverty would have some explanatory power for imprisonment increases. The role of financial resources in a state and imprisonment increases is apparent, both in the positive correlation of average per capita income (INCPC92) and imprisonment (.2777) and in the negative association between imprisonment increases and poverty (−.1355). Here, we are probably dealing with a *facilitating variable* as opposed to a *causal variable*. In other words, wealth did not cause an increase in imprisonment rate, but the availability of resources seems to have made prison expansion possible.

However, Rusche and Kirchheimer (and others) have suggested that there is a strong association between poverty and unemployment, on the one hand, and increases in the rate of imprisonment, on the other. The data found here did not support this thesis, however. The relationship between the unemployment rate (VAR 10) and the increase in imprisonment (VAR 1) was only .1964. Consequently, a state's rate of unemployment, notwithstanding the predictions of Rusche and Kirchheimer, has very little explanatory power in predicting the rate at which imprisonment will increase.

In addition, the percentage of the population who live below the poverty line (VAR 9) and the increase in imprisonment rate (VAR 1) was actually a negative (i.e., −.1400). In short, the factors that explain the variation in the growth of prisons do not include poverty or unemployment.

CONCLUSION

This analysis leaves us with the following question: If the uneven increase in imprisonment in the fifty states over the twenty years studied cannot be explained by variations in the crime rate or other commonly cited socioeconomic or demographic variables, then what does explain the increase? Chapters 5 and 6 look at some political factors that may be relevant.

NOTES

1. Michael Tonry, *Malign Neglect* (New York: Oxford University Press, 1995), p. 79.

2. Georg Rusche and Otto Kirchheimer, *Punishment and Social Structure* (New York: Columbia University Press, 1939).

3. Michael Tonry, *Malign Neglect* (New York: Oxford University Press, 1995), p. 19.

4. Louis Freedberg, "New Jump in Rate of Incarceration for Black Males," *San Francisco Chronicle*, October 5, 1995, p. 1.

5. U.S. Department of Justice, *Sourcebook of Criminal Justice Statistics, 1994* (Washington, D.C.: Bureau of Justice Statistics, 1995), p. 338.

6. U.S. Bureau of the Census, *1990 Census of Population, General Population Characteristics*, United States (CP 1–1) (Washington, D.C.).

5

The "Law-and-Order" Governors and Their Counterparts

CRIME AND POLITICS

It is my argument that the political views of U.S. governors concerning the proper reaction to criminal offenders should be considered one of the most significant factors in determining interstate variations in the rate of imprisonment. Nonetheless, researchers in public policy have done very little analysis in this area. "Crime has become Public Enemy Number 1," according to a recent *Time* essay, and "a bigger concern to most people than joblessness or the federal deficit."[1] How is it that crime could have become such a public obsession when, as shown in the National Crime Survey, the crime rate hit a peak of 41 million offenses in 1981 and has been falling ever since (to around 34 million offenses in recent years)?

Why is it that a recent nationwide poll showed that "89 percent of those surveyed think crime is getting worse,"[2] when even inflated figures in the "reported crime" of the FBI's *Uniform Crime Reports* show significant annual decreases? For example, in 1980 the UCR rate was 5,950 per 100,000 population, yet in 1993, the rate had dropped to 5,482.[3]

In referring to the public's perspective on the contemporary problem of crime in the United States, the *Nation* recently editorialized, "Rarely has political consensus strayed so far from the facts."[4] In other words, there are very few examples where the public view of a social problem is less justified by the realities of the situation than the subject of crime in the 1990s.

The answer to this enigma lies, at least in part, in the political exploitation of public confusion and the fear of crime. This exploitation has come in the form of the innumerable law-and-order campaigns that have been waged for almost three decades—from the mid-1960s, when the first of the baby boomers entered the crime-prone age group, and, predictably, sent crime rates spiraling upward.

One recent study of this problem examined every crime story covered by *Time, Newsweek*, and *U.S. News and World Report* from 1956 to 1991 and concluded "that 'media amnesia' has allowed each new anti-crime crusade to be portrayed as if the preceding ones had not happened."[5] These crusades have been of enormous value to some political candidates. The voters may feel an ill-defined malaise with the way things are going, yet be unable to articulate the causes of this malaise. As Stuart Scheingold has argued: "Criminals provide a convenient target for the anger that is widely felt, but is not quite appropriate to express, with respect to unwelcome changes in race relations, employment opportunities and homelessness."[6]

It has been generally assumed that the beneficiaries of the law and order campaigns have been conservative Republicans. However, it has been recently argued that no political candidate is safe ignoring the crime issue and that every "candidate for public office in the United States this year is unwilling to challenge the prevailing rhetoric and talk reality on crime and punishment."[7] In other words, what was once the exclusive province of conservative Republican political candidates is now more widespread. Concluded one editor, "Both parties now go by the once Republican equation that 'soft on crime' adds up to liberal loser."[8] Despite objections that "the Constitution should not be used to score political points," which came from White House advisors, the Clinton administration proposed a "victim's rights amendment" in the 1996 campaign in order to respond to Republican initiatives in the area of getting "tough on crime."[9]

It was not always the case that political candidates felt it mandatory to take a position on crime. The political benefits of taking a tough law-and-order position has become increasingly apparent over the past couple of decades. As it has evolved, the tough rhetoric has become both more strident and more bipartisan. Perhaps the best example of this evolution is the direction taken by the party presidential platforms of the recent past on the issue of crime.

PARTY PRESIDENTIAL PLATFORMS

The party platforms created for the presidential campaigns of the past two decades have contrasted sharply on the issue of law and order. The Republican platform has unfailingly taken the hard line on crime and encouraged state officials to follow suit. "The most effective weapon against crime," argued the 1980 Republican platform, "are state and local agencies."[10]

In regard to legal reforms that each party considered necessary, the difference was pronounced. In 1984 the Republicans would include in their platform: "The Republican anti-crime agenda: oppose furloughing criminals, re-establish the death penalty, reform the exclusionary rule to prevent the release of the guilty on technicalities, reform cumbersome habeas corpus procedures, implement preventive detention."[11] The Democrats, on the other hand, suggested different reforms for the problem of crime: "We must eliminate elements like unemployment and poverty that foster the criminal atmosphere."[12]

The Republican call for a "war on drugs" was reflected in every recent party platform. In 1976, the party was already calling for mandatory minimum sentences for drug offenders,[13] and it repeated the call in 1980.[14] In 1984 the platform called for a "dramatic increase in the penalties for narcotic offenses,"[15] and in 1988 it demanded both the death penalty for drug traffickers and an "expanded military role in stopping traffickers."[16]

Beyond the death penalty, in 1984 the Republican platform for the first time came up with specific, Draconian suggestions, which many states would later implement. Drug dealers, in the view of the platform, were "domestic terrorists" who deserved capital punishment. Moreover, for the first time, drug users were also targeted.

"User accountability for drug usage is long overdue," said the platform. "Conviction for any drug crime should make the offender ineligible for discretionary assistance, grants, loans and contracts. We urge states to suspend eligibility for a driver's license to anyone convicted of a drug offense." Many states would take their cue from these suggestions. In addition, the widespread use of drug testing was introduced with the line: "We will require federal contractors and grantees to establish a drug-free work place."[17]

The Democrats were somewhat more sanguine in their approach to drugs. "We should make every useful diplomatic, military, educational, medical and law enforcement effort necessary," stated the Democratic platform of 1988, "and it should include comprehensive programs to educate our children at the earliest ages on the dangers of alcohol and drug abuse, readily available treatment and counseling for those who seek to address their dependency."[18] Thus, the solution to the problem of drugs for the Democrats of 1988 was education, prevention and drug treatment; for the Republicans, it was increased law enforcement pressure and government harassment of drug users.

On the subject of guns, the parties took predictable paths. The Republicans consistently assert that they "oppose federal registration of firearms. Mandatory sentences for [the] commission of armed felonies are the most effective means to deter abuse." The Democrats, however, would "support tough restraints on snubnosed handguns" in 1984 and the "enforcement of a ban on 'cop killer' bullets" in 1988.[19]

The Republicans demonstrate a remarkable faith in the ability of government agencies, such as the courts, to resolve the problem of crime,

Table 5.1
Governors of the States Used in This Study with Increase in Rate of
Imprisonment per 100,000 Population and Percentage Increase during Their
Administration

State	Governor	Increase in Imprisonment (rate per 100,000)	(% increase)
1. New Hampshire	Judd Gregg 1989-93	+54	+72%
Maine	John McKernan	+00	0
2. Missouri	John Ashcroft 1989-93	+75	+31%
Kansas	Joan Finney 1990-94	+06	+03%
3. South Carolina	Carroll Campbell 1986-90	+42	+39%
North Carolina	James G.Martin	-02	-02%
4. Delaware	Michael Castle 1985-89	+68	+26%
Maryland	William Schaeffer	+06	+02%
5. Kentucky	Wallace Wilkinson 1987-91	+99	+70%
W.Virginia	Arch Moore/Gaston Caperton	+09	+11%
6. Arizona	Evan Mecham 1987	+39	+14%
CA,UT,NV and NM	average	+06	+03%
7. Louisiana	Buddy Roemer 1988-92	+116	+34%
North Dakota	George Sinner	+11	+19%

whereas the Democrats appear to be hopeful only that the courts can render justice. The platform for the Republicans in 1980 argues: "The existence and application of strong penalties are effective disincentives to criminal actions. Yet these disincentives will only be as strong as our court system's willingness to use them."[20] On the other hand, the Democrats in 1984 suggest, "Our courts should not be attacked for failing to eliminate the major social problem of crime—courts of justice were not designed to do that."[21]

Prison sentences were also discussed by the Republican platforms, which reasoned that "the best way to deter crime is to increase the probability of detection and to make punishment certain and swift. Republicans advocate sentencing reform and secure, adequate prison construction."[22] By 1988, the platform would demand "an end to crime" and what it called a "historic reform of toughened sentencing procedures for federal courts to make the punishment fit the crime." The Democrats thought that sentencing reform should include "diversion programs for first and non-violent offenders" as well as "reform of the sentencing process so that offenders who commit similar crimes receive similar penalties."[23]

The stark contrast between the parties in their platform planks concerning crime began to disappear in the 1992 election. Perhaps Republican success in exploiting the issue brought the Democrats closer to the law and order position. For instance, in the 1988 presidential campaign, George Bush very successfully used the story of Willie Horton to embarrass his opponent, Michael Dukakis. Horton was released from a Massachusetts prison while Dukakis was governor of that state. Horton was later arrested for a brutal rape, and TV ads from the Bush campaign implied that it was Dukakis' fault that people like Horton were free. Horton had actually been paroled under a law passed by Dukakis' Republican predecessor in the Massachusetts state house, and it is very unlikely that Dukakis knew anything about his parole. Nonetheless, political observers considered the ad campaign very damaging to Dukakis.

These national political platforms may well have contributed to the quintupling of the number of U.S. inmates between 1972 and 1993, as the law-and-order theme in national politics inevitably colored state-level politics. Moreover, while national party platforms may have pointed the way, the implementation of prison expansion would be left to those officials directly involved in the operation of state prisons, namely, the state governors.

Seven of these governors, six of them Republicans, presided over extraordinary increases in the imprisonment rate in their state. I will examine their views of crime and punishment and then compare them with their counterparts in contiguous states (see Table 5.1).

NEW HAMPSHIRE AND MAINE, 1989–1993

Governor Judd Gregg served for four years as governor of New Hampshire. During that time (1989–1993), the inmate population of the state increased from 103 inmates per 100,000 population to 157. During the same four years, in the adjacent State of Maine, Governor John McKernan presided over an inmate population that remained unchanged.

Specifically, on the first day of 1989, per 100,000 population, New Hampshire had 103 inmates and Maine had 116. Four years later, Maine still had 116 inmates per 100,000 population, but Judd Gregg's state, New Hampshire, now had 157 inmates per 100,000, an increase of 52 percent.

The crime rate is relatively low in both New Hampshire and Maine (about two-thirds the national average), and their violent crime rate ranks them forty-ninth and fiftieth in the nation.[24] During this time period, the overall rate of reported crime fell in both states by about the same percent (See Table 6.1). New Hampshire experienced a 12 percent drop in reported crime; Maine saw an 11 percent drop.

The demographics of the two states are very similar, nor do their economic and social problems differ much. Why, then, was there such a difference in the use of prisons between 1989 and 1993? It is my argument that the answer lies in the public posture of the state's chief executive officers.

New Hampshire

Judd Gregg's political career seems to have been designed to demonstrate such consistently reactionary positions that no one would question the editorial opinion that "Judd Gregg is devoutly conservative."[25] As a new member of the U.S. Senate in 1995, for instance, Gregg went out of his way to become part of Conservative leader Newt Gingrich's inner circle. When "Gingrich held one of his regular meetings with the cadre of loyalist representatives who would be the core of his conservative band," Gregg was always there.[26] Gregg's major positions as a freshman Senator were to cut the capital tax rate and reduce cuts in defense spending.[27]

Earlier in his career, as governor of New Hampshire, Gregg demonstrated similar political leanings. He made constant calls for broad changes in education, state financial support to attract business, and an end to over-regulation of business.[28] In his first year as governor, Gregg proposed a 9 percent cut in state spending on education (in order to keep down taxes), despite a massive increase in the cost of maintaining an expanding prison population.[29]

He "promised that he would not let a sales tax or income tax slip into the state,"[30] and would later brag that "taxes in New Hampshire are the lowest in the country."[31] "As Governor, he vetoed three bills that would remove the state's 1848 anti-abortion laws from the books,"[32] and promised that he would not support the Freedom of Choice Act.[33] In a dispute involving the separation of church and state, "Gregg argued that the President of Keene State College should be fired because she moved a prayer service off campus at the state supported college."[34] The college president believed that prayer in a public school had been banned by the Supreme Court. Gregg had to know that this area of constitutional law is confusing to public officials and legal scholars everywhere. Nonetheless, he also understood that the polls show widespread public support for prayer in public places, and his call for the president's dismissal was designed to exploit this sentiment.

It is clear from the U.S. Department of Justice data that during Governor Gregg's term, the inmate population grew dramatically, even though the crime rate was falling. The reason for this increase in imprisonment was not an increase in crime but an increase in the rate of imprisonment per crime.

One veteran administrator in the New Hampshire prison system stated at the end of Gregg administration that "the recently revised laws that require minimum sentences [has resulted] in young offenders being imprisoned much longer than before."[35] He went on to argue that "you've got a lot of young kids up there doing time for almost nothing[;] . . . at least 200 are serving time for driving stuff."[36] Thus, the voters of New Hampshire may have been led to believe that their prisons were being filled with murderers and rapists, but their prison administrators spoke of young inmates sent to them for "driving stuff."

Judd Gregg's approach to the problem of drugs best exemplifies his law-and-order perspective. As a congressman in 1987, Gregg wrote an article for the *Congressional Digest* about the solution to the problem of drugs. Consistent with the philosophy of the Republican national platform, he stressed surveillance and law enforcement over education and treatment as the solution to the drug problem. Gregg also argued that every federal agency head should drug test their employees and thereby set an example for others to follow.[37]

Gregg viewed the drug problem as less a social crisis than a law enforcement problem.[38] Despite the fact that under Gregg's administration, New Hampshire prisons lacked the funds to provide any kind of drug and alcohol treatment for inmates,[39] Governor Gregg was able to find special funds to provide additional investigations of drug use in the high schools.[40]

Gregg's call for punitive judges is very similar to that of the Republican national platforms. In addition to Gregg's outspoken support for Clarence Thomas as a Supreme Court justice, he also called for trial court judges who would "get tough" on crime.[41] When Governor Gregg was criticized for nominating New Hampshire judges who were "not up to snuff," his reaction was to state that "they are strong judges who, when they make a decision, are definitive," adding that "when someone is found guilty of a crime, these judges don't hesitate to effectively mete out justice."[42]

When Judd Gregg left the New Hampshire statehouse to accept his seat in the U.S. Senate, he left behind many problems for the prison system. "With the state facing a growing inmate population, the Legislature must fund a master plan for correctional facilities," said the then commissioner of corrections, who noted that there were serious problems with "expanding prison populations and the siting and funding of new facilities."[43]

In order to relieve overcrowding in the prisons, corrections officials began using electronically monitored home confinement to ease overcrowding.[44] In addition, Gregg's successor found it necessary to give the attorney general authority to set up an early release program to ease overcrowding at the state prisons.[45] Before leaving office, Judd Gregg did authorize a 500-bed minimum-security prison, called "Camp Success," which would offer steady work to 150 local workers, and he saved $20 million by converting an old school building rather than building from scratch.[46]

Despite the fact that New Hampshire went through a ten-year prison renovation and expansion program, the flood of inmates sentenced to New Hampshire prisons under Gregg's leadership would still overwhelm the system by the time he left office.[47] Gregg's law-and-order approach led to serious problems in New Hampshire prisons as the crowding and under-staffing grew steadily worse. By 1991, the newspapers would be filled with horror stories about the prisons.

For example, after two inmates were murdered in a New Hampshire prison, the press questioned how one inmate could have been stabbed forty times before correctional officers reached him.[48] While the prison officials took the position that they could not make public the number of in-mates per officer because of "security reasons,"[49] it was estimated that as many as "280 inmates may be watched over by as few as two or three officers."[50] These conditions led to an inmate strike toward the end of Gregg's term.[51]

Conditions in the New Hampshire prisons grew inevitably worse as the state's chief executive insisted on tougher sentences and cuts in state spend-ing. Gregg loved to boast that "New Hampshire remains the lowest taxed state in the country, with the lowest cost of government in the country."[52]

Gregg prided himself in the cutbacks on expenses for state employees, including the elimination of state-paid health care for its employees.[53] How-ever, the restrictions on prison staffing were not without cost. As a news article pointed out: "Prison inmates have flooded U. S. District Court in Concord with more than 250 lawsuits against New Hampshire State Prison over the past 7 years." Included in complaints were the failure of officers to protect prisoners from violence from other prisoners, interrupted access to visits and crowded and inhumane conditions. "What has changed," said a prison spokesman, "is allegations that prisoners feel unsafe, that they are being abused by prison staff and assaulted by other prisoners."[54] Inside the prisons, "inmates and staff have said that the overcrowded prison is rou-tinely understaffed and that is a contributing factor to the violence."[55]

Maine

During the same four years while Governor Judd Gregg was increasing the prison population of New Hampshire by 52 percent, John McKernan was serving as governor of Maine. On the day Gregg was sworn into office, Maine had an inmate population of 116 per 100,000 population—actually higher than the figure in New Hampshire. However, four years later, when New Hampshire had increased its prison population to 157, Maine contin-ued to have just 116 inmates per 100,000. Why did this happen? The answer lies in a comparison of Governor Judd Gregg and Governor John McKernan.

The crime rates in Maine and New Hampshire are very low by national standards. The national average of roughly 5,600 serious offenses per 100,000 population is far greater than the figures in Maine (3,523) and New Hampshire (3,080). During the 1972–1992 period, Maine and New

Hampshire saw increases in the rate of reported crime that were very similar—51 percent in Maine and 54 percent in New Hampshire. Both Gregg and McKernan are Republicans, but that is where the similarity ends. Governor Gregg was a law-and-order governor; John McKernan was not.

"During McKernan's first term in Congress he aligned himself with the Republicans' congressional left wing, voting against the President [Reagan] 50 percent of the time,"[56] which ultimately "attracted charges from the political right that he was "an ultra liberal."[57] McKernan's position on crime and drugs is the direct opposite of that of the law-and-order governors. For example, one of his major concerns about the crime problem involves his support for gun control laws, a position that is not popular in rural Maine.[58]

McKernan did not pursue the war on drugs with the same enthusiasm as Judd Gregg. During his gubernatorial campaign, his opponents pointed out that while serving as a state senator in Maine's legislature, McKernan had provided a key vote that kept alive a measure to decriminalize marijuana.[59] It is possible that his view of the "war" was influenced by the fact that, according to the *Maine Times*, McKernan was "the only gubernatorial candidate to admit to having tried marijuana."[60]

Political realities would eventually catch up with McKernan and he would move toward the conservatives in his party. "With speculation about the 1986 Gubernatorial race focused on him, McKernan gradually began to swing to the right," coming out "for such uncharacteristic causes as a statewide ban on pornography and the death penalty."[61] However, he never approached the law-and-order advocacy of his counterpart in New Hampshire, and during his four years as governor, Maine's imprisonment rate would experience no increase at all.

MISSOURI AND KANSAS, 1989–1993

On the first day of 1989, Kansas and Missouri had virtually identical rates of imprisonment per 100,000 population (Kansas had 232; Missouri, 236). Four years later, however, Kansas had increased its rate by 6 inmates per 100,000 population; Missouri had increased its rate by 75. The crime rate in each state remained very similar, despite the differences in imprisonment usage. Consequently, between 1989 and 1993, the imprisonment rate in Missouri increased about 12 1/2 times faster than the increase in an adjacent state, Kansas. The crime rate in Missouri is about 2 percent higher than the rate in Kansas, and there was very little difference in the changes in the crime rate in each state between 1989 and 1993. Why did the rate of imprisonment increase so much faster in the former than in the latter? My answer lies in the political figures who presided over each of these states during that time.

Missouri

On the day in 1985 when John Ashcroft was sworn in as governor of Missouri, there were 175 inmates per 100,000 population. When he left office eight years later, there were 311 inmates per 100,000 population, an increase of almost 80 percent. However, it was in his second term, from 1989 to 1993, that the larger increase occurred. In that term Ashcroft presided over an increase of 75 inmates per 100,000 population. In Kansas, the increase in prison population during this same four-year period was just 6 per 100,000. Missouri's UCR rate in 1993 was 5,095; for Kansas, it was 4,995.

After John Ashcroft finished his second term as governor of Missouri and ran successfully for the U.S. Senate, an editorial summarized his accomplishments as follows: "Ashcroft's eight years will be most remembered as a time of wholesale cuts in key state services, nearly $1 billion in reductions."[62] However, that editor did not discuss spending on Missouri prisons.

In his eight years, Governor Ashcroft invested $115 million in prison construction, building four new prisons and expanding four more.[63] The prison expansion was so rapid that the Department of Corrections actually leased cells to other states prior to the expansion of the Missouri prison population.[64] However, as the law-and-order atmosphere under Ashcroft began to influence Missouri's criminal justice officials, the prophecy of prison expansion critics, that if built, the prisons would be filled, soon came true. Missouri prisons quickly reached a point where the state was unable to lease out cells to other states, and not long after the end of leasing out empty cells, the problem of overcrowding actually began to appear in Missouri prisons.

The method of financing Missouri prisons did involve a unique approach to imprisonment programs. A private developer built and owns the new prisons; the state leases and operates the prisons under a thirty-year lease. Ashcroft claimed that "this financing package freed an estimated $50 million to fund other state obligations."[65]

However, while Missouri was willing to greatly increase public funds for housing offenders, government housing was not available for everyone. Even while approving prison construction, Ashcroft vetoed a state housing-assistance bill and was sharply criticized by advocates of the homeless and low-income families.[66]

Under Ashcroft, new laws embodying tough sanctions for offenders were passed and increased the capacity for law enforcement to fight crime.[67] The net effect was a rapid expansion of the rate of Missouri imprisonment. The total case load for the Department of Corrections grew from 25,000 to 43,000 during Ashcroft's tenure.[68] State prison funding increased from $87 million to $208 million (139 percent) during Governor Ashcroft's administration, and the number of prison guards rose from 1,400 to 2,700.[69]

State spending on colleges and universities dropped compared to that of other states, and Missouri fell to forty-seventh place in per capita funding of higher education.[70] However, Ashcroft would later boast that he had demonstrated his concern for college students in passing a new law that gave a prison term of not less than ten years for people distributing controlled substances near colleges or universities.[71]

The *St. Louis Post-Dispatch* once argued that in the nationwide war on drugs, Governor John Ashcroft's voice had been one of the "shrillest."[72] Indeed, most of his second inaugural address apparently concerned the topics of drugs and pornography, both "red meat" subjects for the law-and-order right.[73]

Ashcroft's second term would begin with the reintroduction of the death penalty in Missouri[74] (although the state modernized the process by authorizing the Department of Corrections to use lethal injections rather than the gas chamber for executions).[75] The death penalty was also provided for in an omnibus antidrug bill that authorized it for drug-related murders. Ashcroft claimed that "he recognized the need to fight drugs with the latest and best law enforcement strategies,"[76] and under the Ashcroft administration, antidrug funding grew from $19 million dollars in 1985 to $93 million in 1993.[77]

Editorials warned of the "hysteria" in some of Ashcroft's drug proposals,[78] including denying bail to drug offenders, a proposed law that would punish pregnant women who used alcohol or drugs,[79] the stationing of police officers in public high schools to combat drug use,[80] the outlawing of "street gangs,"[81] and revoking the driver's license of anyone convicted of possessing drugs—regardless of whether they were in a car at the time they were caught.[82]

Ashcroft slashed the budget for treating drug abusers and "in addition to the cuts to the Division of Alcohol and Drug Abuse, Ashcroft vetoed funding for two separate residential treatment programs for children whose primary problems are abuse and neglect."[83] Moreover, the *Kansas City Star* would editorialize that recent budget cuts would result in "substandard welfare benefits, overcrowded prisons and the virtual dismantling of traditional mental health programs."[84]

Aside from cutting public spending, Ashcroft also shifted spending from programs that might reduce the demand for drugs to programs that would almost certainly have no impact. For instance, while everyone agrees that pregnant drug addicts can do great harm to their babies, the question of what to do about them is disputed. There is general agreement, however, that medical attention is an important part of the solution.

A pregnant woman with a drug problem might ask herself where to find help in Ashcroft's Missouri. Certainly, help was not available from a medical doctor. Ashcroft's legislation turns all doctors into police informers by "mandating physician identification of alcohol and drug abuse in pregnant women."[85] Why seek out prenatal medical care if you will be turned into the police?

Many of Ashcroft's proposed reforms in drug laws were stopped by the Missouri legislature, which found them too extreme.[86] However, many of his proposals for increasing police powers in dealing with drugs were more successful in the legislature. For example, Governor Ashcroft signed legislation granting full search-and-seizure powers to the Highway Patrol,[87] and, at Ashcroft's urging, "the General Assembly authorized the use of electronic surveillance for gathering evidence of drug-related felonies."[88] Ashcroft also boasts about how he provided the Missouri Highway Patrol undercover officers with "buy money" for undercover operations and encouraged the patrol to purchase high-tech infrared equipment to help officers locate indoor drug-cultivation operations.[89]

The last year for which Missouri imprisonment figures are available is 1993, the year John Ashcroft spent his first year as a U.S. senator. In 1993, the rate of imprisonment fell for the first time since 1979. It may be that the atmosphere in the Missouri criminal justice system was beginning to change and the hysteria that had characterized Ashcroft's Missouri was abating. In any case, more inmates were released from state prisons that year than were admitted. Missouri's prison explosion had come to an end.

Kansas

During most of the Ashcroft administration, Joan Finney served as governor of Kansas. Finney is a Democrat who was elected in the heavily Republican state of Kansas after serving as state treasurer for twenty years.[90] She alienated the voters by opposing the death penalty, which polls showed was widely popular among Kansans. When the state legislature sent her a death penalty bill, she refused to sign it.[91] In speaking to a group of voters about her overall view of crime, Governor Finney stated: "Bigger jails and stiffer penalties are not the solution." . . . We need to bring families together so young people do not turn to drugs and crime."[92]

To emphasize her perspective, Finney singled out a state parole officer for a special award after he had demonstrated a humane and progressive approach to drug and alcohol rehabilitation for his parolees.[93] In addition, she proposed funding for AIDS education and establishing early intervention services centers,[94] and she urged the adoption of "Operation Immunize," a statewide program to vaccinate every child under two years of age.[95]

If these positions served to alienate Finney from the electorate, it appears that the issue of gaming among Native Americans may have been the final straw. She touched off a storm of controversy when she signed compacts with four Kansas tribes approving gaming.[96] The compacts would authorize gambling casinos to be set up by tribes of Native Americans in Kansas. The attorney general, at the direction of the Republican-dominated legislature, sued Finney over the tribe's gaming compact but lost.[97]

Finney's approval rating was estimated to be around 25 percent when she approached reelection.[98] Finney announced her retirement from politics amid much criticism, but she recently announced her candidacy for the Senate seat abandoned by Robert Dole.[99]

THE CAROLINAS

North and South Carolina have a great many social, economic, political and demographic similarities. The crime rate is almost identical, with less than a 5 percent difference. On the last day of 1985, the imprisonment rate per 100,000 population was also very similar; specifically, South Carolina had 294 inmates per 100,000 population and North Carolina had 254. Four years later, however, there was a dramatic difference in the imprisonment rate. South Carolina had increased its imprisonment rate by about 42 percent, to a level of 415 per 100,000, and North Carolina had actually reduced its rate to 250, despite the fact that during these years North Carolina spent a considerable amount of tax dollars on new prison construction.

Reported crime rates had increased in both states during this four years, but the increases were very similar and the rate of crime differed very little at anytime during these four years (see Table 6.1). The social and economic problems of both states remained largely the same, and drug use had shown similar patterns in each state. The most likely event to explain this sudden change in imprisonment rates is the election of Carroll Campbell as governor of South Carolina.

South Carolina

Political leaders who make use of popular prejudices and promises in order to gain power are often referred to as "demagogues." The term has haunted Carroll Campbell's entire political career. On April 27, 1990, a murderer was executed in South Carolina. Governor Campbell and refused to commute this man's sentence, and the media had given the story a lot of attention. On the day before the execution, the governor called a press conference on the steps of the statehouse where he proclaimed a "Crime Prevention Week" and presented the proclamation to the family of the murder victim.[100]

The proclamation may or may not have consoled the family; it certainly did not hurt the image of the law-and-order governor. It was political theater of the kind that Campbell's longtime friend and advisor, Lee Atwater, had always promoted.[101] Atwater, a political advisor for George Bush who was largely responsible for the "Willie Horton campaign," knew well the value of exploiting the voters' fear of crime.

Among many Democrats, the perception of Carroll Campbell has always been that he "plays on the worse fears in people, that he takes advantage of peoples' prejudices over a whole range of issues."[102] Campbell began his political career in 1970 when he served as spokesman for the "Citizens to Prevent Busing Committee" after the U.S. Fourth Circuit Court of Appeals ordered school segregation to end immediately in South Carolina. It was said at the time that Campbell had "demogogued the busing issue for personal political gain"[103] when he led an anti-busing protest to the statehouse.[104]

Political opponents would charge over the next twenty years that in that busing protest, Campbell's speeches helped inflame racial disturbances throughout the state.[105] Although it was said at the time that he had "exploited highly volatile and emotional issues," the actions nonetheless launched his political career as a state senator.[106]

In 1978 Campbell ran successfully for the House of Representatives against a Democratic candidate who was Jewish. Campbell's campaign polled voters in his district and asked how they felt about having "a Jewish immigrant" represent them in Congress.[107] The results of the poll were then released to the press by an obscure third candidate. Campbell admitted that he had conducted the poll[108] but denied having provided the poll results to the other candidate.[109]

In 1986, Campbell ran for governor. Only one other Republican had ever been elected governor of South Carolina in the twentieth century,[110] and two months before the election, Campbell was trailing in the polls.[111] The "race card" had been good for Campbell in the past, and it would prove useful for him again.

At the time, the Confederate flag flew over the statehouse in South Carolina, and blacks had long complained that it was a symbol of the state's onetime dedication to slavery. Sensing that his opponent wanted to avoid the issue, Campbell announced proudly that he would keep "the flag flying because it is part of our heritage."[112] He would carry a large majority of the white vote, but the polls indicated that in fall 1985, he was still trailing in the race. Campbell needed another issue.

Pollsters said that the voters believed Campbell's Democratic opponent would do a better job on education and the environment, but that Campbell would be tougher on crime.[113] Campbell therefore played to his strength. According to the *Atlanta Journal*, Campbell "drove home his tough talk on drugs by taking a much-publicized urinalysis and requiring the same of his campaign aides, promising that such tests would be standard in his administration."[114]

His opponent refused to participate in what became known as the "jar wars" by also having a urinalysis. However, when his opponent railed that Campbell's exploitation of the issue was "McCarthyism," it was viewed by political observers as a mistake since "most of the voters don't remember who McCarthy is."[115] In response to criticism of his "jar wars" technique, Campbell argued: "The only people who ought to worry about a drug test are people who have to worry about how they are going to come out on it."[116] In a close election, Carroll Campbell became the second Republican governor of South Carolina in this century.

Over the next four years, South Carolina would increase the percentage of its population that was imprisoned by over 42 percent,[117] and the population of the state juvenile penal institutions would more than double.[118] Campbell took pride in this fact and, when running for reelection, he would brag about how much tougher South Carolina had become on crime and drugs under his leadership.[119]

Drug policy was indeed toughened under Campbell. During his administration, South Carolina began using mandatory minimum prison terms and no-parole sentences.[120] In addition, laws dealing with drugs and schools were dramatically changed under the Campbell administration. Although the self-styled "education governor" was a disappointment to South Carolina teachers, who saw "their salaries fall to thirty-eighth in the nation (and wound up suing Campbell), Campbell himself believed he had done a great deal to improve South Carolina schools.[121]

For instance, the governor signed a new law increasing the sentence for possessing drugs in school from thirty days in a detention center to a year[122] and signed another bill containing harsher penalties for drug offenses committed within a half mile of schools (e.g., ten years for the sale of cocaine)[123] and also allowing offenders aged fifteen and older to be treated as adults. Under Campbell, policy was changed in the prosecutors' offices concerning the prosecution of drug-addicted mothers, despite the fact that the American Medical Association and the American Academy of Pediatrics opposed the policy and said that the courts and the police had no business going after pregnant women.[124]

A policy to charge woman using drugs during pregnancy with child abuse and murder if the baby died as a result was put into effect under Campbell.[125] Prosecutors in Greenville and Charleston began vigorously pursuing criminal child neglect charges against women whose babies were born with traces of drugs in their system.[126]

The Omnibus Drug Act gives drug traffickers the death penalty, makes it easier for police to seize traffickers' property and creates whole new categories of illegal drugs.[127] "The drug legislation . . . is stuffed with new offenses and penalties to help police and prosecutors fight illegal drugs" and said to be focused at the "casual user."[128] It allows police to seize vehicles "intended for use in drug trafficking"[129] and "gives prosecutor's offices 20 percent of the take in drug seizures."[130]

Campbell was unequivocal in his support for using police to eliminate the problem of drug abuse, which he viewed as a moral failure. He argued: "We must emphasize individual accountability and responsibility. Offering excuses for irresponsible personal behavior is going to encourage irresponsible personal behavior."[131] He would later suggest that "the word will get out before long that this is not a place for people to come who want to sell drugs, and if they do, they'll be dealt with harshly."[132] He took great pride in the "Governor's RAID Team," a task force that he credited for the rapid increase in drug arrests during his administration.[133]

North Carolina

Governor James G. Martin served as governor of North Carolina from 1985 until 1992. The demographics of North Carolina are similar to South Carolina, and the crime rate in the two states differs by less than 5 percent. Nonetheless, when James G. Martin took over as governor in 1985, there were 254 inmates per 100,000 population, and four years later there were fewer: only 250 per 100,000. Why did the imprisonment rate expand rapidly in South Carolina yet drop in North Carolina?

Martin was just the second Republican to become governor of North Carolina in this century.[134] Democrats often refer to him as "one of the most level-headed governors we have had."[135] Before entering politics, Martin was a chemist by training and a professor by trade, teaching at Davidson College.[136]

The extraordinary thing about Martin is that although he did not preside over a large increase in prison inmates, he did preside over a prison construction program that was unprecedented. "In March 1986, as part of a 10 year plan to reduce prison crowding, he called for $203 million to expand the system by 10,000 beds."[137]

There is an expression used about prison construction to the effect that imprisonment grows because we "build and fill." Even James E. Roark, executive director of the North Carolina Center on Crime and Punishment, a nonprofit think tank, warned Governor Martin that "if there is any lesson from other states, it's if you build prisons, you will fill them."[138] But in the absence of a "law and order" governor, that apparently did not happen in North Carolina.

In July 1990 the newspapers reported that "since 1985, North Carolina has spent about $200 million on prison construction—but all of that money has gone toward alleviating crowded prisons by providing more room for about the same number of inmates."[139] Martin continued to show an interest in prison construction, and he "spearheaded a $200 million prison bond referendum [, which was] approved by the voters in 1990."[140] Thus, Martin saw a prison system that was badly overcrowded and did what was needed to be done to alleviate that problem. The new prisons that were built under Martin's leadership were filled with the same inmates who were already serving time, rather than by the drug users and property offenders who were being added to prison populations elsewhere. However, when James Martin left office in 1992, North Carolina had 269 inmates per 100,000, just 15 more than when he had come to office eight years earlier. Despite a massive prison-building program that would improve conditions for inmates, Martin's administration would average an increase in the imprisonment rate of less than 1 percent per year.

DELAWARE AND MARYLAND, 1985–1989

Between 1985 and 1989, while Delaware was increasing its imprisonment rate by 68 inmates per 100,000 population, neighboring Maryland would increase its rate from 285 to 291, less than one-tenth Delaware's rate of increase. The difference in the crime rate in the two states is not unusual and the drug problem is very similar between the two neighbors. However, the differences in the political views concerning law-and-order issues held by the governors who served in each state were very substantial.

Delaware

In 1985, Michael Castle began his first term as governor of Delaware. On December 31, 1984, the eve of his inauguration, Delaware had 263 inmates per 100,000 population. Eight years later, when Castle left office, there were 390 inmates per 100,000 population, an increase of 127 inmates per 100,000. During Castle's first term, the increase of 68 inmates per 100,000 population was the biggest increase during any of the gubernatorial administrations in Delaware between 1972 and 1992.

Delaware's political culture has always been on the conservative side. (For example, more than half of the Fortune 500 companies are incorporated in Delaware.)[141] In fact, when Thomas Carper replaced Castle in the statehouse, he was the first Democrat to be elected governor of Delaware in twenty years.[142] Nonetheless, former deputy attorney general Michael Castle introduced a law-and-order atmosphere in Delaware that had not existed up until his election.

In discussing his position on crime, Castle stated that "once a crime has been committed, I believe that you cannot be too tough."[143] When critics pointed out that during Castle's eight years in office there had been a rapid increase in the school dropout rate, Castle bragged that his term had also witnessed a very rapid increase in the imprisonment rate.[144] It's unlikely that anyone dared to suggest to the governor that perhaps the same people who had dropped out of school were filling the ranks of the new admissions to prison.

In fact, the imprisonment rate increase had been so dramatic that all four of the candidates for the job of replacing Castle as Delaware's governor (including the Republican candidate) promised in their campaign literature that they would either reduce the level of imprisonment or, at least, find alternatives to further incarceration.[145]

What Castle left behind in Delaware when he took his seat in the House of Representatives (where he would become a signer of the "Contract with America") was a state that was, in his words, "a bad place to commit a crime."[146] For instance, Delaware remains one of the few states that still provides the option of hanging as a means of capital punishment,[147] and during Castle's administration, a bill that would have introduced public whipping as a punishment for drug offenders was debated by the Delaware legislature.[148] Moreover, Delaware has numerous methods of cutting the cost of dealing with criminals,[149] one of which is the practice of using inmate labor to build the prisons.[150]

As governor, Castle pumped money into the court system to deal with rising caseloads and pushed for legal changes that would make procedural reforms to speed justice.[151] He signed a bill that made hearsay evidence admissible in some cases and extended the statute of limitations in others.[152] However, while these changes may evidence a tough approach to crime, they were of minor significance in determining Delaware's expansion of imprisonment. However, Castle's new drug laws were significant in that regard.

As a former law enforcement official, Castle believed that social problems like drugs could be cured by the criminal law system. Even as a congressman, Castle would advocate more money for interdicting the supply of drugs, deploying military forces in the war on drugs, and spending less on drug treatment and prevention.[153]

As governor, Castle introduced and signed into law some of the nation's harshest mandatory minimum sentences for drug violations.[154] These laws would lead to an unprecedented crowding of the Superior Court docket, which wound up overflowing with criminal cases, mostly drug prosecutions.[155] Editorials at the end of Castle's term would cite these drug laws as being directly responsible for the imprisonment expansion. Said one, "Delaware's growing prison population was an outgrowth of harsh mandatory minimum sentences for drug violations which Castle signed into law."[156]

Castle may be the quintessential example of a law-and-order political figure who benefited from the crime issue. At the time when he finished his eight years as governor and won election to Congress, Castle was widely considered by the media to be "one of the most successful elected officials in state history."[157]

Maryland

The governor in Maryland during the same time was Democrat William Schaefer, a moderate who had served for fifteen years as mayor of Baltimore, where his "redevelopment efforts made the city a national urban success story."[158] Unlike some of his counterparts, Schaefer did not have much need to carefully watch the polls before making policy decisions. He came into office with an enormous mandate,[159] having won his election with a record margin of 82 percent of the vote.[160]

Schaefer was viewed as a big spender who steered state aid to the poor and homeless, economic development of the cities, and "support from the wealthier subdivisions to the poorer." He argued that "inequality means we all pay for the dropouts, the prisons, the juvenile delinquency, the teen pregnancy."[161] During his first two years in office, it was said of him that "the poor became his constant companions. He [mentioned] them in nearly every speech."[162]

On the subject of crime, William Schaefer could not have been more different than his colleague across the border in Delaware. While Governor Castle of Delaware was saying that he did not believe it was possible to be "too tough on criminals," Governor Schaefer, just a few miles away was quoted as saying: "I happen to be a proponent of when a person [has] served their time, you give [him] a break."[163] Schaefer's primary interest in crime legislation seems to have been banning assault guns,[164] for which he regularly received the opposition of the National Rifle Association (NRA).[165]

Moreover, while it is true that in his first two years, he built new prisons[166] and had the state take over the Baltimore jail and expand its capacity, the result was to relieve overcrowding rather than increase capacity.[167] In fact, after a visit to one prison, Schaefer was so appalled by the conditions that he ordered it closed immediately.[168] On another occasion, Schaefer demonstrated unusual patience during a prison riot, and his restraint was credited for peacefully resolving it.[169]

Schaefer's primary interests in criminal sentencing were to double the number of convicted defendants sentenced to community service rather than incarceration, get tough on domestic violence, increase gun control and crack down on "deadbeat dads" (who owe child support) and drunk drivers.[170]

In addition, Schaefer is given credit for computerizing law enforcement information systems,[171] and he was widely praised for taking an approach to the drug problem that demonstrated "compassion."[172]

KENTUCKY AND WEST VIRGINIA, 1987–1991

Kentucky and West Virginia have a good deal in common in terms of social, economic and political problems. Both have very low crime rates and low rates of imprisonment. Kentucky has a crime rate of 3,223 UCR offenses per 100,000 population; West Virginia stands at 2,609. During the four years from 1988 and 1992, both states experienced an almost identical increase in the reported crime rate (roughly 8 percent). However, the increase in the imprisonment rate was significantly different.

In the period between 1972 and 1992, both states increased their rates of imprisonment by less than the national average of 250 percent. However, between 1988 and 1992 the rates of increase in imprisonment were very different in the two states. West Virginia increased its imprisonment rate by about 7 percent; Kentucky increased by 70 percent.

While the total increase in the rate of imprisonment in Kentucky between 1972 and 1992 was just 172 per 100,000 population, an increase of 99 per 100,000 occurred in a single four-year period, under the Wallace Wilkinson administration. As Kentucky was increasing its prison population by 99 inmates per 100,000 population between 1987 and 1991, the prison population in neighboring West Virginia grew by just 8 inmates per 100,000.

Demographically and culturally, the two states are quite similar. The social and economic systems are similar, as are the problems confronting them. Why should there be such a disparity in the growth of imprisonment? Again, prison expansion can only be understood as an outgrowth of politics.

Kentucky

Wallace Wilkinson was elected governor of Kentucky at a time when the rate of imprisonment was 142 per 100,000 population. Four years later, Kentucky had a prison population of 241 inmates per 100,000 population. The increase was the largest by far of the five administrations during the 1972–1992 period and amounted to a 76 percent increase in four years.

Wallace Wilkinson was a wealthy businessman with no political experience when he ran for governor in 1987.[173] During his administration he would make substantial cuts in the state budget,[174] and minority groups complained that during his administration, the percentage of minorities in the state workforce fell.[175] In regard to crime, Wilkinson introduced a bill that lowered the level of intoxication necessary for a drunk-driving conviction and another that would remove the driver's license of people convicted of drunk driving.[176] Moreover, it is widely believed that the most significant achievement of the Wilkinson administration was the introduction of the lottery to Kentucky.[177]

However, it was in the war on drugs that Wilkinson demonstrated his law-and-order credentials. He was especially eager in his war on marijuana. Wilkinson proudly announced a new effort to fight marijuana growers by finding and destroying the plants and prosecuting those who grew them.

He announced that $3.9 million would be spent on the plan in order to show that "it is absolutely unacceptable to grow marijuana in Kentucky and it is going to be extremely hazardous to those who attempt to do that."[178]

In the same announcement he stated that Medicaid funding in Kentucky for substance abuse treatment at children's facilities would be halted because the state did not have enough money. It was estimated that the treatment cost around $2 million per year.[179]

West Virginia

Governor Arch Moore served three terms as governor of West Virginia. His last two years of service came in 1987 and 1988, and contemporaneous with the first two years of Wallace Wilkinson's administration. He was defeated for reelection by Gaston Caperton, who served from 1989 to 1993.

During the 1987–1991 period, West Virginia saw an increase in reported crime of 8 percent and an increase in the rate of imprisonment of 7 percent. Neither governor advocated prison expansion or a get-tough approach to crime.

Democrat Arch Moore served as governor of West Virginia from 1969 to 1977, and he was elected again in 1985. Moore made substantial efforts at reforming the state's education system,[180] but the state was in desperate financial condition and his plans were thrown off-track.[181] The West Virginia prison system was in such a deplorable state that the inmates held in a state prison that had been built before the Civil War rioted on New Year's Day, 1986, and three people were killed.[182] Nonetheless, Moore kept the institution open and functioning.

It may be suggested that Arch Moore was reluctant to expand the prison population of West Virginia because he anticipated the day he might become part of that expansion. Moore himself was eventually sentenced to five years for taking kickbacks from a contributor who was allowed to get illegal refunds from the state's Black Lung Fund.[183] His popularity with the voters, however, helped him come close to being reelected, even after his indictment.[184] Moore ultimately returned to the state $750,000 of the money he had received,[185] but he nonetheless lost in a close race against Gaston Caperton in his bid for an unprecedented fourth term.[186]

When Gaston Caperton was elected governor of West Virginia the state had a $500 million deficit. On the day he left office, however, the deficit was just $35 million. Caperton passed the largest tax hike in history[187] and was known for his attempt to cut bureaucracy.[188] Editorials gave Caperton credit for cutting government spending, paying off the state's debt, and punishing government mismanagement.[189] However, they also said that Caperton paid a price for pledging not to raise taxes and then raising them as soon as he took office.[190] Nonetheless, Caperton took greatest pride in his efforts to improve education.

Gasper Caperton pledged to revitalize the state's educational system because he believed that education was the key to redirecting the economy.[191] Caperton pressured the West Virginia legislature to increase spending on education, but met with limited success.[192] He is remembered in West Virginia for his school-building drive as well as his attempt to cut the state bureaucracy.[193] His sweeping reorganization package was aimed at the state's declining college and university system.[194]

By the end of his term, Caperton would boast that he had wiped out the state's deficit, created jobs and put a computer in every elementary school classroom in the state.[195] Even *Time* magazine would acknowledge, "Governor Gaston Caperton has introduced an innovative health cost-containment plan for state employees, initiated a radical restructuring of the state's education system and arranged for payment of the state's debt."[196] Unlike his counterpart in nearby Kentucky, Caperton did very little that would expand the rate of imprisonment in West Virginia.

ARIZONA AND CALIFORNIA, UTAH, NEVADA AND NEW MEXICO, 1987

In Arizona between 1972 and 1992, the biggest single increase in the number of prison inmates came during the 1987–1991 period. This is problematic for my purposes here because there were two individuals who served as governor of Arizona during this period. Governor Evan Mecham was elected in 1986 and took office in January 1987. He was impeached and driven from office about fourteen months later; he was then replaced by the secretary of state, Rose Mofford.

However, while the total increase in inmates was greater during this four-year period than during any other gubernatorial administration during the 1972–1992 period, the increase under Mecham was by far the most dramatic.

While the three years of the Mofford administration averaged an increase of 22 inmates per 100,000 population, in 1987, during the single year of the Mecham administration, the increase was 39 per 100,000. In no other year between 1972 and 1992 was there an increase of inmates per capita anywhere close to 39 (the closest was 25 in 1982).

Arizona is bordered by four Western states. The average increase of inmates per 100,000 population for these five states in 1987 was 7 per 100,000. California increased its prison population by 19; Utah, by 2; Nevada actually decreased by 15; and New Mexico increased by 20. As a percentage increase, that translates into an increase of 8 percent for California, 1 percent for Utah, 12 percent for New Mexico and −3 percent for

Nevada. Arizona's increase of 39 inmates per 100,000 population amounted to a 14 percent of its prison population.

Governor Evan Mecham

Evan Mecham was the first U.S. governor to be impeached in fifty-nine years.[197] He had angered a large number of the voters by canceling the state holiday to honor the Reverend Martin Luther King, Jr., although he would later claim he had been motivated by the cost to the state of such a holiday.[198] The legislature impeached Mecham shortly before a recall election could be held. His impeachment for "high crimes and misdemeanors" came as a result of diverting the funds intended for his inauguration to help out his failing Pontiac automobile dealership.[199]

Mecham argued that the pressure for him to resign came from "militant liberals and homosexuals,"[200] and one of Mecham's supporters compared the investigation of the governor to the trial and passion of Jesus Christ.[201] In the years following his impeachment, Mecham remained active in political fringe groups, headed a white supremacist organization called "Constitutionalists' Networking Center"[202] and founded a political party called CURE, which stood for "Constitutionally Unified Republic for Everyone."[203]

Governor Mecham is a good example of how one individual can set an attitude throughout the minions of criminal justice officials which results in a rapid increase in imprisonment. Even though Mecham did not have enough time to preside over an extensive prison-building program, his very presence in the statehouse was enough to bring about a rapid increase in imprisonment levels.

A law-and-order governor can lead a legislative reform of penal codes and sentencing policies or a massive investment in prison facilities. Both moves can ultimately result in a substantial increase in imprisonment. However, quite aside from these long-term projects, a governor can almost instantly create a "law-and-order mood" among police, prosecutors, parole officers, probation officers, judges and parole boards that can also bring about a substantial increase. These individuals exercise enormous discretion over individuals who are involved in crimes and can quickly implement a punitive approach to the crime problem that results in a rapid increase in prison population. Such appears to have been the case during Evan Mecham's ill-fated fourteen-month regime.

The extremism of Mecham's political views was well known to the Arizona voters when he was elected. "Mecham supported and was supported by members of the John Birch society,"[204] and is on record as stating "that President Eisenhower supported socialist policies."[205] Mecham further argued that "federal policies regarding education, homosexuals, welfare programs and separation of church and state were the same symptoms that led to the fall of the Roman empire."[206] Early on in his administration his derogatory remarks angered blacks, homosexuals, women, journalists, legislators and politicians. He cost the state millions in revenue from canceled conventions and companies that decided not to locate in Arizona.[207] He also argued that the United States might have become "too much of a democracy."[208]

Mecham's election to the statehouse created a tough-on-crime atmosphere. In his book, Mecham claimed that the greatest achievement of his administration was his success at "persuading the Legislature to pass stronger criminal laws and to match federal dollars for funding stronger law enforcement to combat drugs."[209] Even editorials that were critical of Mecham conceded that he had "succeeded in beefing up that state's drug abuse prevention efforts."[210] However, the speed with which Arizona prisons grew under the governor clearly demonstrates that he did a lot more than simply toughen existing laws. Mecham also created an atmosphere of encouragement to those who favored greater punitiveness in the handling of criminals.

Even mainstream Arizona Republicans would launch a campaign to fight a takeover by a new conservative group led by televangelist Pat Robertson and Evan Mecham.[211] However, the law-and-order advocates in the Arizona criminal justice system took solace in Mecham's view of crime and shared in his view that "America's eventual moral collapse will again prove that any society that will not protect itself from moral decay will be destroyed by it."[212]

Apparently, the governors of Arizona's neighboring states of California, Nevada, Utah and New Mexico did not perceive the same level of "moral decay," nor did they send the same "get-tough" message to their criminal justice systems.

LOUISIANA AND NORTH DAKOTA, 1988–1992

Thus far I have examined states with extraordinary growth in imprisonment rates and compared their governors with the governors of contiguous states with low growth. In each instance, the political rhetoric concerning law and order differed between the governors. Would the same pattern hold up if we were to compare the states with the highest and lowest number of inmates per 100,000 population?

The state with the highest rate of imprisonment is Louisiana; the state with the lowest is North Dakota. While there are polar differences between these two states, it may be informative to examine the administration that presided over the most rapid growth in Louisiana and compare it to the contemporaneous administration in North Dakota.

In Louisiana between 1988 and 1992 there was an increase in the imprisonment rate of 116 inmates per 100,000 population; in North Dakota, the increase was 11. However, the significance of this difference is lessened when we look at the percentage increase. Louisiana increased its rate of imprisonment by 34 percent, and North Dakota had an increase of 19 percent. While North Dakota continued to have a low rate of crime and Louisiana continued to have a high rate of crime, both states experienced roughly similar increases in their reported crime rates during these four years.

The most apparent reason for this difference in the increase in imprisonment rates was the political views of the governors who served in these two states between 1988 and 1992.

Louisiana

On the day in 1988 when Buddy Roemer took over as governor of Louisiana, the state prisons had 346 inmates per 100,000 population. During the Roemer administration, a four-year period in which crime both nationwide and in Louisiana remained relatively stable, the governor presided over a 34 percent increase in the size of the inmate population, a larger increase than in any other modern Louisiana gubernatorial administration. At the end of Roemer's four-year term, there were 462 inmates per 100,000 population in Louisiana, which ranked the state highest in the nation.

By the time of Roemer's reelection campaign, he could confidently promise the voters that, as "a law and order candidate," he would "lead the Legislature in creating the toughest crime package in America."[213] There were few who would question his credentials for making such a claim.

Roemer had rushed into the race for governor in the final three weeks of the campaign, gaining major newspaper endorsements and showing well in a widely televised multicandidate debate.[214] Roemer knew he was getting into a very difficult job, and he faced it with little in the way of a mandate. (He took office even though a majority of the voters opposed him.)[215]

How did a state that "was on the verge of bankruptcy" in 1988 and saw painful cutbacks in many state agencies find the money to expand its prison population so dramatically?[216] Roemer knew that on taking office, he was destined to "implement a drastic austerity program designed to severely curtail social services."[217] As one of his first official acts, he "asked the legislature to give him authority to cut state departments" in the "economically depressed" state.[218] He almost immediately proposed a budget that would reduce state aid to schools by nearly 20 percent[219] and would later propose the closing of half the state's public colleges in order to balance the state budget.[220] Ultimately, over four years, Roemer would "cut 16,000 people from the state's 75,000 person payroll."[221]

While others would write of Buddy Roemer that he had "assembled power that makes Huey Long look like a piker," the governor went even further.[222] Commenting on his own power in Louisiana, Roemer stated, "I am the most powerful Governor in America."[223]

Buddy Roemer established a law-and-order atmosphere in Louisiana that was to have a pronounced impact on the state's approach to imprisonment. While a member of Congress, Roemer had frequently voted with the Reagan White House and had provoked the wrath of Democratic leadership on more than one occasion.[224] By the time Roemer announced that he was switching parties and running as a Republican, the *Times-Picayune* claimed that the "very conservative congressman had voted with Reagan republicans more than any other House Democrat."[225]

During his first term as governor, Roemer would demonstrate a consistent law-and-order philosophy, and by his second year, Roemer had "addressed a joint session of the House and Senate and pointed to continued budget pressures and to some areas that should be given more money, including state police, corrections and anti-drug initiatives."[226] Roemer himself claimed that his investment in prisons was forced on him by federal court orders that compelled the state to reduce prison overcrowding.[227] Moreover, a crime panel that he had appointed had concluded that more money must be spent on Louisiana's prison system.[228]

During his administration, Roemer provided special funds to the city of New Orleans to fight crime,[229] signed a bill giving prosecutors extraordinary powers to get into the bank accounts of suspected drug offenders,[230] and, after four other states had refused their permission to build a new federal prison, Roemer volunteered a site in Louisiana for that purpose.[231]

Perhaps Roemer's most unusual demonstration of his commitment to law and order came with the exercise of the governor's power to commute sentences. Gilbert Rideau is an inmate in Louisiana prison system who acquired a measure of renown by publishing a newspaper about prison life. After serving some thirty years, Rideau was recommended for parole by the governor's pardon board. However, Roemer refused to follow the recommendation and grant clemency, and Rideau remains in prison.[232]

The following year, the board again recommended clemency for an inmate by requesting that the governor commute the man's death sentence to life without the possibility of parole. Dalton Prejean killed a man when he was a minor and was given the death penalty. As *Time* magazine saw it: "Prejean was remorseful and semi-retarded, with partial brain damage and a history of abuse as a child. He was also a black juvenile convicted by an all-white jury."[233] Because of his youth at the time of the crime, the pardon board recommended that the governor commute the death penalty to life without the possibility of parole.

Again, Roemer refused.[234] In an unusual twist, the governor phoned Prejean just an hour before his execution and informed him that his execution would be good for society: he then called the media to inform them of the conversation. Prejean was executed,[235] and the governor's public image of being tough on crime reached legendary proportion, even today when "acts of clemency have become a rarity in a political environment that rewards unflinching toughness."[236]

Even the *Times-Picayune* editorial cautioned Roemer to tone down his law-and-order rhetoric, including his call for "chain gangs for prisoners," which, the editorial claimed, were "just too harsh for the people Roemer needs to attract after runoff."[237] In addition, Roemer promised to call out the National Guard to patrol the streets of New Orleans and conduct drug raids,[238] describing the problems of that city as more like a "war" than a "crime problem."[239] However, it was the image of himself as a "crime warrior" that had proven so politically successful for Roemer, and it was not something he would lightly give up.

North Dakota

When George Sinner took office as governor of North Dakota in 1988, the state had an imprisonment rate per 100,000 population of just 57. When Sinner left office four years later, the rate had grown to 68 and remained the lowest in the nation. In Louisiana, the rate had grown by 116 inmates per 100,000 population during the same four years; in North Dakota, it had grown 11 per 100,000. Clearly, North Dakota has not believed in imprisonment as a cure for social ills.

Sinner, an ex-seminarian who was said to place his emphasis on human services and education,[240] was required to make an immediate $21 million reduction in the state budget as soon as he took office.[241] However, his second budget reflected a large increase in spending, with the lion's share going to human services.[242] His final budget called for another increase of $150 million.[243]

Governor Sinner never achieved great popularity with the voters, despite the respect he enjoyed among political commentators. Editorials said of Sinner's style that his greatest fault was his failure to realize that "good government is usually poor politics."[244] He never appealed to the passions that Buddy Roemer and the other law-and-order governors had awakened in their constituents and he never experienced their political success.

NOTES

1. "Crime: Safer Streets, yet Greater Fear," *Time*, January 30, 1995, p. 12.
2. Ibid.
3. U.S. Department of Justice, *Sourcebook of Criminal Justice Statistics, 1994* (Washington, D.C.: Bureau of Justice Statistic: 1995), p. 305.
4. Katrina vanden Heuvel, "String 'Em Up," *Nation*, November 21, 1994, pp. 599–600.

5. Robert Elias, "Official Stories: Media Coverage of American Crime Policy," *The Humanist* 54, No. 1 (January–February 1994): 3–8.

6. Stuart A. Scheingold, "Politics, Public Policy and Street Crime," *Annals of the American Academy of Political and Social Science* (May 1995): 155–168.

7. vanden Heuvel, "String 'Em Up."

8. Ibid.

9. "Periscope," *Newsweek*, June 10, 1996, p. 4.

10. John L. Moore, ed., "Republican Party Platform," *Historic Documents of 1980* (Washington, D.C.: Congressional Quarterly, 1981), p. 593.

11. Margaret C. Moore Thompson, ed., "Republican Party Platform," *Historic Documents of 1984* (Washington, D.C.: Congressional Quarterly, 1985), p. 3.

12. John L. Moore, ed., "Democratic Party Platform," *Historic Documents of 1980* (Washington, D.C.: Congressional Quarterly, 1981), p. 2.

13. Robert A. Diamond, ed., "Republican Party Platform," *Historic Documents of 1976* (Washington, D.C.: Congressional Quarterly, 1977), p. 629.

14. Moore, "Republican Party Platform," p. 594.

15. Thompson, "Republican Party Platform," p. 605.

16. Hoyt Gimlin, ed., "Republican Party Platform," *Historic Documents of 1988* (Washington, D.C.: Congressional Quarterly, 1989), p. 656.

17. Ibid.

18. Hoyt Gimlin, ed., "Democratic Party Platform," *Historic Documents of 1988* (Washington, D.C.: Congressional Quarterly, 1989), p. 562.

19. Gimlin, "Republican Party Platform," p. 656; Gimlin, "Democratic Party Platform," p. 562.

20. Moore, "Republican Party Platform," p. 594.

21. Margaret C. Moore Thompson, ed., "Democratic Party Platform," *Historic Documents of 1984* (Washington, D.C.: Congressional Quarterly, 1985), p. 562.

22. Thompson, "Republican Party Platform," p. 605.

23. Gimlin, "Republican Party Platform," p. 656; Gimlin, "Democratic Party Platform," p. 562.

24. John Allard, "S.C. Violent Crime Rate 5th in U.S," *Columbia State*, August 11, 1991.

25. "Two New Hampshire Women Show Limits Moderate Republicans Face," *Baltimore Evening Sun*, April 15, 1995, p. 2a.

26. "Gingrich Allies," *Washington Post*, December 20, 1994, p. A:1.

27. Deborah Snyder, "Gregg Unveils Cure for U.S. Economy," *Concord Monitor*, July 21, 1992.

28. Felice Belman, "Gregg Upbeat in Assessment of State," *Concord Monitor*, January 8, 1992.

29. Robert Rothman, "Spending Revolt in New Hampshire," *Education Week* 8, No. 22 (February 22, 1989): 8.

30. Kathleen Burge, "Gregg, Rauh Exchange Fire over Records," *Concord Monitor*, Oct 26, 1992, p. E8.

31. Ibid.

32. Kathleen Burge, "Two Men, Two Styles," *Concord Monitor*, November 1, 1992.

33. "Gregg, Rauh Spar in Debate," *Concord Monitor*, October 13, 1992.

34. Hayward, Mark, "Sturnick Fires Back," *Keene Sentinel*, May 3, 1991.

35. Roger Talbot, "Guards Union Warning: NH Prison Staffing Dangerously Low," *New Hampshire Sunday News*, May 12, 1991.

36. Ibid.

37. Judd Gregg, "Is the Administration's Approach to Federal Employee Drug Testing Sound?" *Congressional Digest* 66 (May 1987): 148.

38. John Milne, "Anti-Drug Effort Belies Seething Social Crisis," *Boston Globe*, November 5, 1989, p. 1.

39. Kevin Landrigan, "Drug, Alcohol Treatment in Prison Wanted," *Nashua Telegraph*, December 16, 1988.

40. "Drug Fight in N.H. Schools," *Boston Globe*, April 11, 1990, sec. 32X, p. 4.

41. Donn Tibbetts, "Arnold, Fitzgerald Nominated to Superior Court," *Manchester Union Leader*, November 19, 1992, p. C14.

42. Ibid.

43. Donn Tibbetts, "Powell: Plan for Prisons," *Manchester Union Leader*, November 18, 1992, LAW 117:C6.

44. Roger Talbot, "Bracelets Part of Push to Ease Overcrowding at State Prison," *Keene Sentinel*, October 27, 1991.

45. Pat Grossmith, "Governor Gives AG a Say in Early Release of Felons," *Manchester Union Leader*, July 1, 1993.

46. Paula Tracy, "Safe or Not, Prison Expected to Be Hard Sell," *Manchester Union Leader*, December 14, 1990.

47. Donn Tibbetts, "Prison Inmates Go to Boot Camp," *Manchester Union Leader*, February 23, 1990.

48. Gerry Davies, "Group: Prison's Problems Are Isolated," *Concord Monitor*, September 19, 1991.

49. Ibid.

50. Roger Talbot, "Guards Union Warning: NH Prison Staffing Dangerously Low," *New Hampshire Sunday News*, May 12, 1991.

51. Gerry Davies, "Inmates Strike Is On," *Concord Monitor*, September 23, 1991.

52. Donn Tibbetts, "State Has $21M Surplus," *Manchester Union Leader*, October 1, 1992.

53. Donn Tibbetts, "Gregg: Great Year for World, Not NH," *Manchester Union Leader*, December 31, 1991.

54. Pat Hammond, "State Prisoners Flood U.S. Court with Complaints," *New Hampshire Sunday News*, March 8, 1992, 30:E7.

55. Gerry Davies, "Group: Prison's Problems Are Isolated," *Concord Monitor*, September 19, 1991.

56. Nancy Perry, "McKernan," *Portland Press Herald*, May 26, 1986.

57. *Maine Times*, October 17, 1986, 53:B8.

58. "Foes' View of Social Positions Similar," *Portland Press Herald*, May 30, 1986, p. G6:29.

59. "Jock McKernan," *Maine Times*, October 24, 1986.

60. *Maine Times*, October 17, 1986, 53:B8.

61. Perry, "McKernan."

62. Will Sentell and John A. Dvorak, "Ashcroft Philosophy," *Kansas City Star*, January 2, 1993.

63. Robyn Burnett et al., *A Working Missouri: The Ashcroft Years* (Jefferson City, Mo.: n.p., 1992), p. 85.

64. Ibid.

65. Ibid.

66. Victor Volland, "Advocates for Homeless Criticize Veto by Ashcroft," *St. Louis Post Dispatch*, July 15, 1990, D8:2.

67. Burnett et al., *A Working Missouri*, pp. 85, 81.

68. Ibid., p. 85.

69. Ibid., p. 87.

70. Sentell and Dvorak, "Ashcroft Philosophy."

71. Burnett et al., *A Working Missouri*, p. 78.

72. Bill McClellan, "Did Ashcroft Kin Go to Pot?" *St. Louis Post Dispatch*, January 22, 1992, A3:1.

73. Kathryn Rogers, "Ashcroft Takes Oath of Office, Urges Fight on Drugs and Porn," *St. Louis Post Dispatch*, January 10, 1989, A1:4.

74. Thomas A. Engelhardt, "Another Re-Inauguration," *St. Louis Post Dispatch*, January 10, 1989, C2:3.

75. Burnett et al., *A Working Missouri*, p. 82.

76. Ibid., p. 77.

77. Ibid., p. 74.

78. "Hysteria and Hope over Drugs," *St. Louis Post Dispatch*, November 27, 1989, p. B2:1.

79. Robert Manor, "Drug Use and Pregnancy," *St. Louis Post Dispatch*, November 18, 1989, B1:2.

80. "Police to Be Stationed at 12 City Schools," *St. Louis Post Dispatch*, January 3, 1992, A1:2.

81. Virginia Young, "Anti-Drug Provisions Get Axed," *St. Louis Post Dispatch*, February 16, 1990, A1:6.

82. Tim Bryant, "Plan Would Revoke Drug Users' Licenses," *St. Louis Post Dispatch*, November 23, 1989, A1:3.

83. "Lawmakers: Vetoes Show Otherwise," *Springfield (Missouri) Daily News*, October 16, 1986.

84. Sentell and Dvorak, "Ashcroft Philosophy."

85. Burnett et al., *A Working Missouri*, p. 80.

86. Terry Ganey, "Ashcroft's Drug Bill Fails Again," *St. Louis Post Dispatch*, May 16, 1992, A1:4.

87. Burnett et al., *A Working Missouri*, p. 79.

88. Ibid., p. 78.

89. Ibid., p. 77.

90. Vicki Allen, "Former Kansas Governor to Run for Dole Seat," Reuters News Service, June 6, 1996.

91. Andrea Stone, "Voter Backlash Nipping at Governor's Heels," *USA Today*, January 31, 1994, p. 8.

92. Wen Smith, "Post People," *Saturday Evening Post*, November 1, 1995, p. 12.

93. Karen Rurhmen, "Kansas Parole Officer Recieves a Welcome Surprise," *Corrections Today* 56 (June 1, 1994): 80.

94. Julie Roverner, "Governor's Speeches Address Health Care Crisis," *Nation's Health* 22 (April 1, 1992): 11.

95. Intergovernmental Health Policy Project, "State Health Notes" (2021 K Street NW, Suite 800, Washington, D.C.).

96. Elaine Schroeder, "Iowa and Potawatomi Approved for Gaming," *News from Indian Country*, May 31, 1993.

97. Joan Morrison, "Kansas Court Rules Indian Gaming Out of Its Jurisdiction," *Lakota Times*, February 2, 1994, p. PG.

98. Thad Beyle, "Pete Wilson for President," *State Government News* 38 (January 1, 1995): 25.

99. On Finney's intentions to retire, see Stone, "Voter Backlash Nipping at Governor's Heels."

100. Schuyler Kropf, "Woomer Makes a Last Bid for Life," *Charleston News and Courier*, April 26, 1990.

101. John Monk, "Lt. Gov. Mike Daniel Is Getting Tough," *Charlotte Observer*, October 12, 1986.

102. Henry Eichel, "Congressman Campbell Means to Win," *Charlotte Observer*, October 12, 1986.

103. Ibid.

104. Jerry Adams, "GOP's Campbell Has Learned How to Win," *Columbia State*, October 19, 1986.

105. Clark Sunratt, "Unrepentant Mitchell Goes on the Offensive," *Columbia State*, October 3, 1990.

106. Eichel, "Congressman Campbell Means to Win."

107. Ibid.

108. Ibid.

109. Adams, "GOP's Campbell Has Learned How to Win."

110. Jerry Adams, "New GOP Chairman Can Run Party," *Columbia State*, January 18, 1987.

111. Jerry Adams, "Governor's Race a Tossup, Polls Show," *Columbia State*, September 7, 1986.

112. Fred Grimm, "Gubernatorial Campaign Is Taking Some Mean Twists," *Miami Herald*, October 21, 1986.

113. Adams, "Governor's Race a Tossup, Polls Show."

114. Hunter James, "Anti-Semitism and Drug Testing Are Hot Topics," *Atlanta Journal*, October 12, 1986.

115. Fred Grimm, "Gubernatorial Campaign Is Taking Some Mean Twists," *Miami Herald*, October 21, 1986.

116. Ibid.

117. Ibid.

118. John Allard, "Beasley Backs Boot Camps," *Columbia State*, November 3, 1995.

119. Andy Brack, "Campbell Makes Bid for 2nd Term," *Charleston News and Courier*, April 24, 1990.

120. Chris Sosnowski, "Operation Weed and Seed," *Columbia News and Courier*, July 12, 1992.

121. Dawn Hinshaw, "S.C. Teachers Suing 'Education Governor,'" *Columbia State*, August 28, 1992.

122. Jeff Miller, "School Crimes Targeted," *Columbia State*, June 19, 1990.

123. Jeff Miller, "Safe Schools Act," *Columbia State*, April 5, 1990.

124. Ken Garfield, "Babies Addicted; Moms Face Jail," *Charlotte Observer*, November 11, 1990.

125. Frank Heflin, "Charleston Plan Saving Unborn Babies from Drug Addiction," *Columbia State*, June 4, 1990.

126. Martin Melendt, "Moms on Drugs: Addicts or Criminals?" *Spartanburg Herald-Journal*, November 25, 1990.

127. Cindi Ross Scoppe, "Campbell OKs Tighter Drug Law," *Columbia State*, June 26, 1990.

128. Ibid.

129. Ibid.

130. Ibid.

131. Sid Gaulden, "Quarter of Mothers Used Drugs, Alcohol," *Charleston News and Courier*, October 24, 1991.

132. Scoppe, "Campbell OKs Tighter Drug Law."

133. Richard Chesley, "Drugs Blamed for Rise in Crime," *Columbia State*, April 22, 1989.

134. Steve Riley, "Martin Turns Fiery on Stump," *Raleigh News and Observer*, October 25, 1990.

135. Bill Krueger, "The Governor Left Out in the Cold," *Raleigh News and Observer*, December 26, 1992.

136. William Swett, "Scientist-Candidates Win in a Few Races," *Physics Today* 38 (January 1985): 92–93.

137. Van Denton, "Compromise Could Fuel Prison Building Boom," *Raleigh News and Observer*, July 2, 1990.

138. Ibid.

139. Ibid.

140. Ibid.

141. Richard Sandza, "Times Next Battleground," *Newsweek*, July 10, 1989, p. 31.

142. Robert Davis, "The New Governors," *USA Today*, November 5, 1992, p. A12:1.

143. Ann Stewart, "Candidates Want a Biggger Bite Out of Crime," *Wilmington Sunday News Journal*, October 4, 1992.

144. Ibid.

145. Ann Stewart, "Next Governor to Attack Crimes Roots," *Wilmington Sunday News Journal*, October 4, 1992.

146. Stewart, "Candidates Want a Biggger Bite Out of Crime."

147. Kurt Heine, "In Del a Choice of Noose or Needle," *Washington Post*, August 18, 1991, p. A5:1.

148. Mark Nardone, "Castle Inks First Set of Child Abuse Laws," *Dover State News*, July 11, 1992.

149. Stewart, "Candidates Want a Biggger Bite Out of Crime."

150. Nancy Kesler, "A Look at Lasting Impressions," *Wilmington Sunday News Journal*, January 3, 1993.

151. Milo Geyelin, "Legal Beat: Clogged Docket," *Wall Street Journal*, December 23, 1991, p. B6:2.

152. Nardone, "Castle Inks First Set of Child Abuse Laws."

153. Stewart, "Candidates Want a Biggger Bite Out of Crime."

154. Kesler, "A Look at Lasting Impressions."

155. Geyelin, "Legal Beat: Clogged Docket."

156. Kesler, "A Look At Lasting Impressions."

157. Mark Nardone, "Castle Coasts to Win," *Dover State News*, November 4, 1992.

158. Sandy Banisky, "The Schaefer Legacy," *Baltimore Sun*, January 18, 1987.

159. John Frece, "New Lawmakers View Schaefer's Way," *Baltimore Sun*, December 10, 1986.

160. John Frece, "Action Memo to State Bureaucracy from Schaefer," *Baltimore Sun*, October 6, 1986.

161. Peter Jensen, "Schaefer Calls Himself a Healthy Duck," *Baltimore Sun*, January 17, 1991.

162. Thomas W. Waldron, "Schaefer's First Two Years," *Baltimore Sun*, January 9, 1989.

163. Doug Birch, "Schaefer Backs 'Break' for Those Who Serve Time," *Baltimore Sun*, December 21, 1989, NIN 13:C12.

164. Richard Tapscott, "Gun-Control Bill Clears Key Hurdle in MD House," *Washington Post*, March 27, 1994, p. B3:5.

165. "Gov Builds Reputation," *Washington Times*, January 14, 1991.

166. Waldron, "Schaefer's First Two Years."

167. Peter Jensen, "Schaefer Unveils Agenda," *Baltimore Sun*, January 19, 1991.

168. Richard J. Margolis, "Our Closet Youth Institutions," *New Leader* 71 (March 21, 1988): 16–17.

169. Bonnie Angelo, "Musical Chairs in Maryland," *Time*, August 26, 1991, p. 21.

170. Dan Casey, "Schaefer Wants Change, Not Cost," *Annapolis Capital*, January 14, 1993.

171. Paul W. Valentine, "Crime War," *Washington Post*, January 8, 1994, p. C3:1.

172. Howard Schneider, "Schaeffer Urges 'Compassion' in Drug Plan," *Washington Post*, February 1, 1990, p. B2:3.

173. Richard Wilson, "Wilkinson Pleased with Achievements," *Louisville Courier-Journal*, October 6, 1991.

174. Tom Loftus, "U.S. Won't Prosecute Wallace Wilkinson," *Louisville Courier-Journal*, August 2, 1995, p. 1B.

175. Fran Ellers, "Affirmative Action: A Look at Kentucky's Experience," *Louisville Courier-Journal*, October 10, 1995, p. 1A.

176. Gil Lawson, "Lawmakers Send Bills on Drunken Driving to Governor," *Louisville Courier-Journal*, February 22, 1991, GOV 28: G5.

177. Bob Johnson, "Bluegrass State Poll," *Louisville Courier-Journal*, March 27, 1995, p. 1A.

178. Gil Lawson, "State and U.S. to Fight Pot-Growing," *Louisville Courier-Journal*, July 17, 1990, LAW 68: G14.

179. Ibid.

180. Tom Mirga, "West Virginia Governor Signs Massive Reform Measure," *Education Week*, 7, No. 39 (1988): 22.

181. Matt Rothman, "Economic Paralysis Could Stop Arch Moore Cold," *Business Week*, November 30, 1987, pp. 86–94.

182. David Wilkinson, "Tourist Captivated by Condemned Prison," *L.A. Times*, November 26, 1995, p. A24.

183. Anita Manning, "Across the U.S.: News from Every State," *USA Today*, November 8, 1995.

184. Joe Urschel, "Shockjock for High Office," *USA Today*, March 24, 1994, p. 12.

185. Sally Lee, "Across the U.S.: News from Every State," *USA Today*, January 30, 1995.

186. Eloise Salholz, "Of Debuts and Dead Heats: A Miracle Worker Falls," *Newsweek*, November 21, 1988, p. 1.

187. Nancy Mathis, "WVa Lawmakers Hike Taxes, Cut School Funds," *Education Week* 8, No. 20 (February 8, 1989): 11.

188. S. C. Gwynne, "Selling Hope in West Virginia," *Time*, May 22, 1989, p. 37.

189. Michael Schroeder, "Can Anybody Govern West Virgina?" *Business Week*, December 4, 1989, p. 40.

190. Maralee Schwartz, "No Taxes Pledge Boomerangs on W.Va. Governor," *Washington Post*, May 10, 1992, p. A6:1.

191. Mary Crystal Cage, "Reeling from Budget Woes, Faculty Flight, and Political Inaction," *Chronicle of Higher Education* 35, No. 23 (February 15, 1989): 19.

192. Nancy Mathis, "WVa Hikes School Aid," *Education Week* 8, No. 30 (April 19, 1989): 7.

193. Gwynne, "Selling Hope in West Virginia," p. 37.

194. Mary Crystal Cage, "West Virginia Governor Wins Approval of Sweeping Changes in Education," *Chronical of Higher Education*, April 19, 1989, pp. 21, A28.

195. Debbie Howlett, "Taxes Are Key to Governors' Races," *USA Today*, May 12, 1992, A6:2.

196. Gwynne, "Selling Hope in West Virginia," p. 37.

197. Margaret Carlson, "He's Back," *Time*, April 23, 1990, p. 24.

198. James E. Ashbrook, "Stevie Wonder Returns to State after MLK Controversy," *Los Angeles Sentinel*, January 25, 1995.

199. Louis Sahagun, "The Survival Instincts of a Bulldog," *Los Angeles Times*, October 21, 1995, p. A1.

200. Margaret Bernstein, "Mecham on the Griddle," *Black Enterprise*, 18, No. 8 (March 1988): 21.

201. "No Comment Department," *Christian Century* 105, No. 13 (April 20, 1988): 390.

202. Joy Press, "An Explosion of Hate," *Newsday*, March 3, 1996, p. 33.

203. Stephanie Saul, "Militias Vent Rage at Governor," *Newsday*, February 19, 1996, p. A8.

204. *Time*, September 29, 1986, p. 35.

205. Ibid.

206. "Up in Arms in Arizona," *New York Times*, November 9, 1987, p. 50.

207. Ibid.

208. Ibid.

209. Evan Mecham, *Impeachment* (Phoenix, Ariz.: 1989), p. 64.

210. "When Evan Mecham Talks, Arizona Shudders," *Business Week*, September 28, 1987, p. 110.

211. Richard Bruner, "GOP Mainstream Fights Right Wing," *Christian Science Monitor*, March 29, 1989, p. 8.

212. Ibid.

213. Joan Treadway, *New Orleans Times-Picayune*, November 2, 1994.

214. Joseph G. Dawson, *The Louisiana Governors: From Iberville to Edwards* (Baton Rouge: Louisiana State University Press, 1990).

215. Lance Hill, "The Curious Rise of Buddy Roemer," *The Nation*, March 12, 1988, pp. 333–336.

216. Tyler Bridges, "The Candidate for Governor," *New Orleans Times-Picayune*, September 20, 1995.

217. *The Nation*, March 12, 1988, pp. 222–226.

218. Sandra Gregg, "The Yuppie Governors of Dixie," *U.S. News and World Report*, March 28, 1988, p. 24.

219. Peter West, "Roemer Seeks to Pare School Budget," *Education Week*, May 18, 1988, p. 10.

220. Mary Crystal Cage, "LA Public Colleges Fear the States Budget Struggle Will Lead to More Campus Cuts," *Chronicle of Higher Education*, May 31, 1989, p. A15.

221. Frank Trippett, "The Roemer Revolution," *Time*, June 13, 1988.

222. Ibid.

223. Ibid.

224. "Buddy Roemer," *Baton Rouge Morning Advocate*, September 8, 1991.

225. Jack Wardlaw, "Roemer Switch Expected for Years," *New Orleans Times-Picayune*, February 7, 1991.

226. Carl Redman, "Governor Preaches Cooperation," *Baton Rouge Morning Advocate*, April 17, 1989.

227. Ed Anderson, "Buddy Roemer Says Management Changes to Be Made in LA Prisons System," *New Orleans Times-Picayune*, July 25, 1989, B1:1.

228. "Crime Panel asks Buddy Roemer to Seek Money for Prisons," *New Orleans Times-Picayune*, June 29, 1989, B4:1.

229. Ed Anderson, "Roemer Said State Will Give Another $2 Million to New Orleans to Fight Crime," *New Orleans Times-Picayune*, September 21, 1990, B1:6.

230. Ed Anderson, *New Orleans Times-Picayune*, July 3, 1990, B3:5.

231. Ed Anderson, *New Orleans Times-Picayune*, October 25, 1989, B1:5.

232. Ed Anderson, "Roemer Says No to Clemency for Inmate News Editor," *New Orleans Times-Picayune*, February 25, 1989, B5:1.

233. Walter Shapiro, "A Life in His Hands," *Time*, May 28, 1990, p. 23.

234. "Roemer Says He Won't Halt Prejean Execution," *Baton Rouge Morning Advocate*, May 15, 1990.

235. "Roemer Called Prejean, Said Death Penalty Served Society," *New Orleans Times-Picayune* May 19, 1990, LAW 43:E9.

236. Shapiro, "A Life in His Hands," p. 2.

237. Iris Kelso, Commentary, *New Orleans Times-Picayune*, September 3, 1995, B9:1.

238. Alfred Charles, "Roemer Says He'll Send Troops into N.O.," *New Orleans Times-Picayune*, October 1, 1995, A24:1.

239. Jack Wardlaw, *New Orleans Times-Picayune*, March 8, 1995, B4:1.

240. Mike Dorsher, "Sinner: Seminary to the Statehouse," *Bismarck Tribune*, January 15, 1989.

241. Bill Hanson, "Governor's Office Struggles Over Cuts," *Bismarck Tribune*, August 24, 1988.

242. Tracy Shatek, "Sinner Asks 11 Percent Bigger Budget," *Grand Forks Herald*, December 7, 1990.

243. Mathew Cecil, "Sinner Budget Bumps Tax Hikes," *Fargo Forum*, December 19, 1992.

244. Phil Harmeson, "Many of Sinner's Efficiency Moves Nothing New," *Bismarck Tribune*, December 18, 1988.

6

How the Prison Population Grew

One of the oddities of the U.S. prison system is the variety of ways in which it is funded and utilized by different governments. More than 90 percent of all inmates are in prisons that are owned and operated by state governments. (The other 10 percent are either in federal or privatized institutions.) "Prisons in the U.S. are paid for at the state level of government out of state correctional budgets, but prison populations are determined by the number of prisoners referred by local officials and the lengths of sentences imposed at the local level."[1] Those who use the service of prisons are not the ones who have to worry about paying for the service. Therefore, every day countless offenders are prosecuted by locally elected prosecutors and sentenced to state prison by locally elected judges who have little or no concern about how those prisons are funded.

Between 1972 and 1992, every state had an increase in the rate of imprisonment, with a national average of around 250 percent, but with enormous variation from one state to the next. Moreover, the social variables that are frequently associated with imprisonment—rate of reported crime, homicide rate, poverty, percent of population that is African-American, rate of unemployment, age of the population, and drug arrests—were not very good predictors of increases in imprisonment rates. Still, certain states increased imprisonment rates thirteen times more than certain others.

The processes through which rates of imprisonment were increased between 1972 and 1992 show many similarities from one state to the next, but they also show some unusual variations. Here we will examine various theories on how prisons grow. We will analyze the "build and fill" theory of prison expansion as well as the impact of political patronage. The rather considerable influence of the war on drugs will also be examined, as will the impact on imprisonment rates attributable to formal penal code reform. Finally, we will look at the effect of changing political attitudes toward crime and punishment on the "informal processes" that help determine imprisonment levels.

"BUILD AND FILL"

One school of thought argues that the very existence of prison capacity automatically leads to increases in levels of imprisonment. That is, new cells never stay empty very long. Therefore, even a needless increase in prison capacity will inevitably increase the number of inmates. There is, in effect, a kind of "Parkinson's Law that suggests that the prison population will simply expand to fill available capacity."[2]

This perspective was best summed up by a Justice Department study done by Kenneth Carlson and colleagues, which concluded that "new space finds its own occupants."[3] Specifically, Carlson and colleagues stated: "As a matter of history, this study has found that state prison populations were more likely to increase in years immediately following construction than at any other time, and that the increase in the number of inmates closely approximates the change in capacity."[4] That study suggested that the increase in imprisonment was not immediate; rather, "there was a two year lag time between the construction of a cell and its being filled."[5]

New prison construction is almost always undertaken in response to some kind of "crisis" situation precipitated by years of increases in overcrowding. Sometimes the crisis is touched off by violent, well-publicized prison riots that call attention to deplorable conditions. More often, however, prison conditions are brought to the attention of federal courts and result in court orders concerning the conditions in existing prison facilities. It is well known that "after Attica in 1971 . . . no region of the country has been unaffected by federal, and occasionally state, court orders to eliminate substandard conditions of confinement."[6]

However, court orders to alleviate overcrowding (or, in the absence of court orders, prison construction bond issues) ordinarily come only after the overcrowding problem has become acute. Thus, the process of creating the overcrowding is often a gradual evolution that begins long before prison construction proposals are issued.

Clearly, the presence of empty, state-of-the-art prison facilities can encourage a criminal court judge to incarcerate a defendant who may otherwise get probation. In some cases, however, new prisons continue to be built, and there is very little subsequent change in the imprisonment rate as the new cells are used simply to replace the old ones. Moreover, much of the growth in imprisonment rates occurs long before any new prison construction.

An increase in a state's rate of imprisonment does not necessarily require the construction of new prisons, as there are many other ways in which the inmate population of a state can grow. For those interested in "getting tough on crime," substantial increases in the imprisonment rate can be achieved long before any new construction begins. These changes can either be accomplished as an outgrowth of formal legislative changes dealing with sentencing or achieved through informal measures, which are more often the most significant influence.

If the number of sentenced inmates increases before new construction begins, where do the new inmates go? State officials have taken numerous approaches to this problem. For instance, prison administrators can decide on their own to use gymnasiums as dormitories, thereby increasing prison capacity. Correctional authorities can authorize double-celling and thereby double their capacity in one move. Triple-celling has become commonplace, and the idea of "warm-bed shifts," wherein one bed is used in shifts by two inmates, has actually been discussed in some states.

Inmates can be shipped out to other states where cells have been rented for them by the sending state; or sentenced inmates can be held in unused county jail cells. Abandoned military bases can be quickly converted into prison facilities by executive order. Minimum security facilities can be upgraded to medium or maximum security and the minimum security inmates can be transferred to newly purchased and modified hotels and motels. It is only after all this emergency space has been exhausted that the overcrowding reaches "crisis" levels and the state is compelled to begin construction of new facilities.

It is therefore possible for a governor to build no new prisons and still preside over a massive increase in imprisonment rates. Evan Mecham served just fourteen months as governor of Arizona, not nearly long enough to launch a prison construction program. However, during his tenure, there was an unprecedented increase in the number of inmates in that state, which was unmatched by far by any previous administration or any of the four contiguous states.

James G. Martin, on the other hand, presided over the construction and opening of a major period of prison expansion in North Carolina. During Martin's eight years as governor, however, there was almost no increase in the imprisonment rate. While Martin modernized North Carolina's prisons, he did not greatly increase their capacity nor preside over a growth in the rate of imprisonment. Therefore, increasing the number of prison buildings will not necessarily lead to an increase in the rate of imprisonment, nor will an increase in the rate of imprisonment always result in the addition of new prison buildings. What other factors, then, are most significant for increasing growth in imprisonment rates?

POLITICAL PATRONAGE

One study of prison construction noted the political implications of advocating expanded prison construction. "Local jobs and future political loyalties," it concluded, "are created by floating big construction contracts for new prisons and jails."[7] Political leaders, that study concluded, consequently may be able to find advantages in proposing large prison expansion projects.

In 1996, there was something of a construction boom in prisons. The federal government constructed twenty-six new prisons; the states constructed ninety-five. The total number of new beds built was around 104,000, and the total cost of the construction was in the area of $7 billion.[8] There has never been a study of the amount of political action committee (PAC) money that comes from either the construction companies that receive these prison building contracts or the construction unions that benefit from the many jobs involved. A third political force, the unions of correctional officers that will run the prisons, has also been ignored by researchers.

Recent media reports, however, have referred to a growing amount of patronage in this area[9] and the growing number of small towns that are actively competing with one another to attract new prisons.[10] Moreover, a study by the Edna McDonnell Clark Foundation on the "current prison-building binge" analyzed the impact of the "corrections-industrial complex" and raised the question of political patronage.[11]

However, trying to explain the prison boom in terms of political largesse is a case of trying to explain a variation with a constant. First of all, there has always been patronage to be dispensed through large state construction contracts—it did not begin in the last two decades. Second, assuming that the temptation of patronage is equally present in all states, why would half the states expand prisons at over twice the rate of the other half? Moreover, why would some states expand prisons at thirteen times the rate of others? Patronage may be a necessary component of explaining recent prison expansion, but it is certainly not a sufficient explanation.

THE INFLUENCE OF THE "WAR ON DRUGS"

The war on drugs has probably not changed the pattern of drug use in the United States very much, but it has had a significant impact on prisons. In 1981, the percentage of new inmates admitted to state prisons who were drug offenders was 7.7 percent. By 1989, however, it had grown to 29.5 percent, and the number of prison commitments for drug offenses had grown sixfold, from 11,487 in 1981 to 87,859 in 1989.[12] By 1992, of all new admissions to state prisons, over 30 percent were for drug offenses.[13]

However, because drug offenders generally spend less time in prison than other offenders, the rate of prison admissions for drug offenses will naturally be lower than the rate of prison inmates who are drug offenders. For instance, on any given day in 1996, inmates serving time for drug offenses constituted less than 25 percent. Therefore, the war on drugs can account for a part of the overall increase in imprisonment, but certainly not all of it.

More important, the question remains why some states waged a war on drugs so much more vigorously than others. Clearly, it is not because of a lack of drug offenders in any state (no state today has "shortage" of drug offenders). The most responsible estimates are that there are 30 to 40 million people who still use an illegal drug at least once a year. There are about 18 to 35 million regular marijuana users in the United States, 5 to 10 million cocaine users, and 5 million heroin users.[14] Despite the billions of dollars spent on the war on drugs, the National Institute on Drug Abuse estimated that at best, we incarcerate one-eighth of the country's hard-core cocaine and heroin abusers.[15] Therefore, even an exponential increase in incarceration of drug offenders would still affect only a very small percentage of all users. Even with an estimated 300,000 drug offenders in prisons and jails nationwide, probably less than 1 percent of all drug offenders are behind bars. It is reasonable to assume that in every state there is a virtually endless supply of drug offenders for criminal justice officials to employ for continued prison expansion.

Consider the data in Tables 6.1 and 6.2. The twenty-five states with the highest rate of increase in imprisonment had an average of 293 drug arrests per 100,000 population in 1992. In the twenty-five states with the low increases, the rate was 259, or 11 percent lower. Moreover, since a virtually endless number of drug arrests can be made by police in any state, the question remains: with or without a war on drugs, why was there such variation in imprisonment rate increases among the fifty states?

INMATE INCREASES THROUGH POLITICAL ATMOSPHERE

It is my argument that it is the political leaders and the impact on a state's atmosphere that lead to increases in imprisonment rates. In turn, rapid increases in imprisonment rates lead to overcrowding, which can touch off a "crisis" that results in prison construction programs. These changes are typically reflected in both the formal and the informal processes of dealing with crime. While the informal processes can be the more important of the two and involve numerous minions of the criminal justice system, the formal processes usually involve the reform of sentencing laws in the penal code.

Table 6.1
Percentage Increase in Rate of Imprisonment, Crime Rate, Homicide Rate and
Rate of Drug Arrests: Low-Increase States

	% INCREASE IN Imprisonment	UCR	hom	drug arrests
26. WI	290	46	4.4	192
27. NV	270	6	10.4	560
28. NM	253	36	8.0	220
29. IA	251	56	2.3	116
30. IN	235	45	7.5	110
31. OK	228	74	8.4	284
32. KS	225	56	6.4	223
33. CO	215	6	5.8	228
34. KY	210	44	6.6	315
35. VA	207	39	8.3	285
36. WY	200	48	3.4	121
37. TN	185	94	10.2	241
38. UT	185	34	3.1	190
39. MD	175	34	12.7	599
40. ME	162	51	1.6	187
41. TX	153	83	11.9	366
42. FL	155	55	8.9	506
43. MN	150	29	3.4	126
44. NE	140	64	3.9	253
45. WA	150	31	5.2	220
46. ND	130	46	1.7	66
47. GA	110	109	11.4	272
48. OR	105	15	4.6	346
49. NC	82	118	11.3	376
50. WV	55	81	6.9	88
average increase	181%	52%	6.7	260

Source: Adapted by Joseph Dillon Davey from U.S. Department of Justice, Sourcebook of
Criminal Justice Statistics, 1993 (Washington, D.C.: Bureau of Justice Statistics, 1994).

Formal Measures: Penal Code Reforms

Each state's penal code is subjected to dozens of proposed "reforms"
every year, and even though most die in subcommittees, many are still
passed into law. The law-and-order attitude that drives increases in sentence severity is an outgrowth of the political environment. Members of
"sentencing commissions" can take a lenient, progressive view of punishment in their reports to state legislatures or a "get-tough" view involving
Draconian reforms. They do not make their judgments unaffected by the
prevailing political winds.

Legislators, when reviewing the recommendations of these commissions,
can read polls that show a growing fear of crime, which makes the tough
approach politically popular, or they can read criminological treatises,
which conclude that prison expansion does little good to reduce crime. In
recent years, however, the treatises have been largely ignored in favor of

Table 6.2
Percentage Increase in Rate of Imprisonment, Crime Rate, Homicide Rate and
Rate of Drug Arrests: High-Increase States

		% INCREASE IN Imprisonment	UCR	hom rate*	drug arrests*
1.	DE	690	7	5.0	334
2.	AK	435	24	9.0	101
3.	IL	435	52	7.4	101
4.	AZ	430	18	8.6	383
5.	NY	430	38	13.3	683
6.	LA	423	93	20.3	309
7.	NH	420	54	2.0	162
8.	VT	401	54	3.6	86
9.	MA	400	21	3.9	254
10.	RI	370	5	3.9	281
11.	MT	355	43	3.0	129
12.	OH	350	35	6.0	91
13.	CT	349	42	6.3	571
14.	MI	340	4	9.8	297
15.	HI	325	32	3.6	325
16.	AR	325	119	10.2	256
17.	ID	320	16	2.9	175
18.	MO	320	29	11.3	269
19.	SD	305	40	3.4	61
20.	CA	305	5	13.1	839
21.	NJ	301	31	5.3	600
22.	SC	300	80	10.3	430
23.	MS	295	137	13.5	178
24.	AL	294	126	11.6	188
25.	PA	293	43	6.8	233
average increase		368%	46%	7.7	293

* drug arrest rates and homicide rates are per 100,000 population

Source: Adapted by Joseph Dillon Davey from U.S. Department of Justice, Sourcebook of
   Criminal Justice Statistics, 1993 (Washington, D.C.: Bureau of Justice Statistics, 1994).

numerous studies that show that being "soft on crime" is the political kiss
of death.

Despite the fact that the United States has had the most severe penalties
of any industrialized nation for a long time, during recent decades, sentences have generally become much more severe in virtually every state.[16]
The early part of these changes was detected by one study that concluded
in 1978. Herbert Jacob and his colleagues conducted an extensive study of
legislative reforms in criminal law over the thirty-one-year period from
1948 to 1978. Jacob studied the changes made by state legislatures and
city councils across the United States during this period.

In summarizing the findings, Jacob stated:

"All levels of government responded to the crime problem by passing new laws.
Sometimes they decriminalized certain behavior but more often they enlarged the

scope of prohibited behavior and increased the penalties that could be levied against the offenders. The most significant legislation was passed during the last years of our study. This legislation removed, reduced, or eliminated the discretion that judges and parole authorities had previously exercised over the length of the sentence that convicts had to serve.[17]

The pattern Jacob and his colleagues recognized would increase during the decade following the study. Specifically, state after state would pass determinate sentencing laws and, for a steadily increasing number of offenses, these sentences would become mandatory.

Mandatory Sentencing. Many states have enacted "mandatory sentence" laws in the past two decades. These laws took discretion away from judges and parole boards and mandated jail or prison time for a wide variety of offenses. As early as 1983, forty-three states had mandatory prison sentences for one or more violent crimes, and twenty-nine states and the District of Columbia required imprisonment for some narcotics offenses.[18]

The constitutionality of one type of mandatory sentence was challenged in a Texas case where a defendant had been convicted of a third property offense. Two of the offenses had involved the improper use of a credit card and the third involved a bad check. Although the total amount of the three offenses involved only $228 and no violence was involved, the Texas court was required, under a mandatory sentence law, to give the defendant life in prison.

The appeal of this sentence was based on the argument that this Draconian sentence was a violation of the due process clause and the cruel and unusual punishment clause of the Eighth Amendment. The U.S. Supreme Court disagreed. The Court upheld the constitutionality of the law, finding that it was possible for the defendant to make parole in twelve years and that this possibility made the punishment something less than "cruel and unusual."[19]

A final point about mandatory sentences should be made. It is widely believed that these laws explain the explosion in prison populations. Criminologist Dianna Gordon, for instance, argued that manditoriness has had a significant impact on both the likelihood of imprisonment and on sentence length.[20] However, recent research has cast some doubt on this assertion. P. J. Langan, a statistician for the Bureau of Justice Statistics, did a detailed analysis of prison populations in 1974 and 1986 and found that the offense distributions documented in the 1974 and 1986 inmate surveys were essentially unchanged.[21]

In other words, the chances of a prison sentence following arrest rose for all types of offenses between 1973 and 1986, not just for those targeted by mandatory prison sentence laws, including sexual, violent, drug and weapons offenses. Violent and other offenses targeted by mandatory sentencing laws have not grown as a percentage of prison admissions, as was expected when the mandatory sentences were passed.

Determinate Sentencing. The practice of "indeterminate sentencing" was begun in the early 1950s in California. Most of the other states followed suit. In the mid-1970s California dropped indeterminate sentencing for a more determinate form known as "presumptive sentencing." This change attracted widespread attention, both in the popular media and in scholarly journals.

Soon afterward, many other states began considering similar reforms.[22] Criminologist Jay Livingston points out, "As the public's belief in rehabilitation of prisoners declined, state legislatures and the federal government as well began to move toward fixed or determinate sentences."[23]

The change from indeterminate to determinate sentencing meant that the time for which an individual is sentenced will be determined by the nature of his or her crime, as opposed to his or her behavior once being incarcerated. A burglar who might receive "one to five" years in prison under an indeterminate sentencing system may receive three years' flat time under a determinate system. Under indeterminate sentencing laws, the exact length of confinement is typically determined, not by a judge at the time of sentencing, but by parole and prison officials based on their judgment of the speed of the person's rehabilitation process while in prison.[24]

Determinate sentences can be fixed by legislators. Of course, there exists in this situation the opportunity for legislators to find some political advantage in showing their constituents how tough on crime they can be. One legislator in California went so far as to introduce a bill that would provide the death penalty for thirteen-year-olds.

It has been suggested that the new determinate sentences will increase the amount of time served by the average inmate.[25] There are, however, others who have argued that under the indeterminate system, prisoners will actually serve more years than they did with specific term sentences.[26] Still others have concluded that there probably is no difference in the average time served under a determinate or indeterminate system.[27] Langan's study supports this third position. He concluded that the length of the average sentence did not change between 1973 and 1986—a time period during which states were abandoning indeterminate for determinate sentences.[28]

Probation and Parole. Another common explanation for the increase in the imprisonment rate is the idea that probation has been severely cut back in recent years. However, Gordon argued to the contrary, that while imprisonment rates have increased, the growth in nonprison penalties is even greater.[29] Moreover, Joan Petersilia found that in California, the number of probationers has increased even faster than the number of prisoners.[30] Actually, both sides of this debate appear to have some merit. The use of probation as a sentence has been cut back, but there are still more probationers today than ever before. In 1970, "slightly more than half of

all offenders sentenced to correctional treatment were placed on probation."[31]

By 1987, 26 percent of persons convicted of a Crime Index offense were
given probation alone. Another 22 percent were given jail time and probation.[32] Therefore, a total of 48 percent of all those convicted were given
some kind of probation, while the other 52 percent were not. Nonetheless,
even with a smaller percentage of defendants being given probation, the
increase in the overall volume of arrests, prosecutions and convictions resulted in a record 2.52 million state and federal probationers in 1990.[33] In
other words, while the percentage of defendants who received probation
fell, the volume of convictions rose so rapidly that the number of probationers rose.

According to Langan, the nation's probation population increased by 96
percent between 1974 and 1986.[34] Parole has also gone through major
changes, but again those changes do not appear to have increased the
prison population. In 1977, nearly 72 percent of those discharged from
prison exited as a result of a parole board decision; in 1985, 43 percent
were released by a parole board; that is, a larger proportion of inmates
served their full sentence before release.[35]

Finally, despite the reduction in the percentages of inmates in many states
who are granted parole, it should be noted that there are more people on
parole today than ever before. The rate of persons on parole per 100,000
adult residents in 1979 was 138; by 1990, it was 287.[36] Since 1980, rates
of growth in probation caseloads have been similar to rates of prison population growth.[37] Today, three out of every four offenders under correctional control are currently supervised in the community.[38] The amount of
legally authorized discretion over probationers and parolees that is exercised by criminal justice personnel can have a significant impact on rates
of imprisonment.

Informal Processes: Discretion in Criminal Justice

The most important influence on the rapid expansion of prisons in the
United States during the last two decades appears to be informal changes
in the system of criminal justice, which grow out of a new attitude toward
punishment. The amount of discretion exercised by street-level bureaucrats
in the criminal justice system is a major, driving force in the increase in
rates of imprisonment. Long before legislators change the penal codes or
the public votes on prison bond issues, the number of inmates can be substantially increased by a much less formal process. Researchers have shown
little interest in this area, possibly because of the difficulties with empirically
measuring the process.

It is indeed rare that a governor or a legislature will announce that tax
dollars are going to be spent on constructing new prison space just in case

the new cells should one day become needed. Prison construction almost always follows critical overcrowding. The decision to increase the number of inmates in a prison system is most often made by a great many low-level apparatchiks in a subtle, evolving process.

In other words, the data suggests that the initial problem of prison over-crowding grows out of a change in attitude among the minions of the criminal justice system who make the majority of decisions about prison use. So much of prison use depends on their decisions that a 1992 study of the problem concluded that "the resulting pattern is so decentralized and disaggregated that no individual or level of government feels responsible for determining prison population policy."[39]

For instance, will a trial court judge exercise the discretion to give a convicted offender a prison sentence or probation; a long sentence or a short one? Where the legislature has taken away discretion with a man-datory sentencing system, the question becomes whether the judge will find the defendant guilty beyond a reasonable doubt in a case where the judge feels the sentence is unfair and inappropriate. Will the judge find the de-fendant guilty of a lesser included offense—perhaps a misdemeanor—in order to avoid an unfair sentence? In fact, so many judges are now refusing to even handle drug cases that impeachment proceedings against numerous individuals have been discussed in Congress.[40]

It is not only the criminal court judge who decides to send an individual to prison. It is also the prosecutor, who may decide to accept a guilty plea to a lesser charge in exchange for a sentence of probation or a short jail stay. What is the political atmosphere that makes the deputy district attor-ney reject a plea-bargain and decide to ask for a long prison sentence of a convicted felon; or, for that matter, to prosecute the case in the first place, rather then, say, dismiss it in exchange for an agreement to join a drug therapy program?

What view will probation officers take about the behavior of their pro-bationers, and what recommendation will they make when writing their presentence reports? Will parole boards grant early release to inmates or return them for another year of prison?

Consider the case of parolees sent back to prison at the discretion of their parole officers. Keep in mind that for every inmate in the United States today, there are three others under correctional control in the community, either on probation or parole.[41] Parole officers can return a parolee for technical violations of parole, such as missing meetings, or they can wait until there has been some serious transgression. Much is left to their dis-cretion, and the impact should not be underestimated. The percentage of all prison admissions is severely impacted by the policies of parole officers.

For instance, Todd Clear's study found a most surprising figure in regard to parole violations. "Over half the admissions in some states," Clear found, "are revocations of probation or parole."[42] Moreover, the National

Corrections Reporting Program found that in 1992, of the 415,000 state prison commitments, over 127,000 were parole revocations. In California in a very short period of time, the percentage of parolees who were sent back to prison went from under 20 to over 60 percent. This was not an outgrowth of changed behavior of parolees so much as it was a changed approach taken by the California parole officers in the political atmosphere of the 1980s. These are numbers that can have a serious impact on the rate of imprisonment for a state.

The same political atmosphere that causes probation and parole officers to take a lenient or harsh view of minor violations of parole will also influence deputy district attorney judgments about plea-bargains and probation officers writing presentence reports for criminal court judges. For that matter, that same political atmosphere will influence every police officer faced with the choice of making an arrest or overlooking a minor offense.

There are about 600,000 police officers in the United States today. They routinely make discretionary decisions about when to make an arrest and when to refrain. (One study found that there is one arrest made for every five "arrest situations.")[43] Most of these decisions involve low-level offenses that will most often lead only to probation and that clog the system. When probation caseloads are too overcrowded to add any more probationers, most will be released by the court with a fine. However, others will be incarcerated, further adding to the overcrowding problem.

POLITICAL INFLUENCES IN PRISON GROWTH

Alfred Blumstein concluded that in the last couple of decades, "[C]ontrol over sanction policy [came] out of the criminal justice system into the open political arena, and opened the door for changes in legislation and in practice that have contributed to the uncontrolled growth of prison populations that characterized the late 1970s and the 1980s."[44] Those changes in "legislation and practice" were the consequences of changing political attitudes toward crime.

Moreover, Zimring and Hawkins concurred with Blumstein: "The major explanation of the prison population expansion of the 1980s is the change in policy rather than a change in the population or in the character of crime,"[45] and "the major influence on future prison population movements will be the direction of changes in the severity of penal policy."[46] Unfortunately, changes in penal policy are also increasingly dependent on political pressures and less and less dependent on rational analysis by social scientists or criminal justice professionals.

Alfred Blumstein put it simply: "It would be most desirable to find ways to take the issue of punishment policy out of the rabid political arena, where the conditions under which the debate occurs can lead to the enactment of much irresponsible policy."[47] These discretionary decisions about the fates of criminal offenders are made in a political atmosphere that can change rapidly. Zimring and Hawkins speculated that a governor's view of crime and punishment has a significant impact and that "a get-tough executive attitude with an emphasis on accountability may lead to more diligent and efficient performance on the part of criminal justice agencies."[48]

This appears to be what happened in the states I studied. There, the evidence strongly suggests that it was the political atmosphere created by a state's chief executive—and the impact of that atmosphere down the line to the minions of criminal justice professionals—that most significantly increased a state's rate of imprisonment. The attitude toward punishment taken by the million or so personnel in the criminal justice system can change very rapidly and have dramatic effects on the rate of imprisonment in any given state.

The influence of a governor in the process of increasing imprisonment rates does not seem to be an outgrowth of his or her legal authority to authorize either prison construction or penal code reform. It appears to lie more in the governor's attitude toward punishment—which is conveyed to the people who exercise discretion over the lives of criminal offenders.

It is my argument here that in the states where the executive created an atmosphere of law and order, prison populations exploded, whereas in the states where the atmosphere was less intemperate, the populations grew slowly. Moreover, this happened with little regard to new prison construction. A good example of this is in North and South Carolina. On the last day of 1985, the imprisonment rate per 100,000 population was very similar in these two states. Four years later, however, there was a dramatic difference between the imprisonment rates. South Carolina had increased its imprisonment rate by about 42 percent, while North Carolina had actually reduced its rate somewhat. Reported crime rates had increased in both states during this four years, but the increases were very similar and the rates of crime differed very little at anytime during these four years (see Table 6.1). The social and economic problems of both states remained largely the same, and drug use had shown similar patterns in each state. The event most likely to explain this sudden change in imprisonment rates is the election of Caroll Campbell as governor of South Carolina and of James G. Martin as governor of North Carolina.

James G. Martin built far more prison cells than Governor Campbell, but he did not increase the rate of imprisonment. Martin was also a Republican, but Democrats often referred him as "one of the most level-headed governors we have had."[49] Under Martin, North Carolina actually spent a great deal of money on prison improvements and modernization, yet there was almost no increase in the rate of imprisonment. In July 1990 the *Raleigh News and Observer* reported that "since 1985, North Carolina has spent about $200 million on prison construction—but all of that money has gone toward alleviating crowded prisons by providing more room for about the same number of inmates."[50]

As governor of South Carolina, Carroll Campbell actually had very little authority to mandate anything, let alone a massive increase in the imprisonment rate. The state's leading newspaper observed that "it has never been a secret that South Carolina was a weak governor state"[51] and that "almost every other state has given its governor more authority than South Carolina has."[52] For at least seventy years, studies have urged that South Carolina "give its governor more power to run the state so that the people know who is in charge. But the South Carolina legislature has kept much of the power for itself, with the rest doled out to the 123 part-time boards and commissions that oversee state agencies."[53]

If the governor's legal authority was as circumscribed as this suggests, how can the rapid prison growth be attributed to anything his office did during that first four years? The answer is in the attitude toward punishment that a governor can convey.

Campbell sent an extraordinarily tough law-and-order message to the South Carolina criminal justice system. He dismissed out of hand the view that crime and drug abuse were an outgrowth of social problems and argued that it was all simply attributable to "moral failure." "We must emphasize individual accountability and responsibility," he argued. "Offering excuses for irresponsible personal behavior is going to encourage irresponsible personal behavior."[54]

His attitude was that getting tough would "send a message" and cause the crime problem to go away. Said the governor about his Draconian suggestions: "Maybe the word will get out before long that this is not a place for people to come who want to sell drugs, and if they do, they'll be dealt with harshly."[55] His message was not lost on South Carolina's criminal justice personnel.

In other words, Martin's State of North Carolina improved prison facilities, but in the absence of the kind of law-and-order rhetoric that came from the statehouse in South Carolina, Martin's tenure (even with new prison facilities) saw no growth in imprisonment rates. Specifically, between January 1, 1986, and January 1, 1990, while the state of South Carolina saw its imprisonment rate per 100,000 population grow from 294 to 416, North Carolina saw its rate actually drop, from 254 to 250.

What did the citizens of South Carolina get in return for this enormous investment in prisons? What does the current research indicate about the social costs and benefits of increasing imprisonment rates? Chapter 7 examines these questions.

NOTES

1. Franklin E. Zimring and Gordon Hawkins, *The Scale of Imprisonment* (Chicago: University of Chicago Press, 1991), p. 211.

2. Alfred Blumstein, "Prisons," in James Q. Wilson and Joan Petersilia, eds., *Crime* (San Francisco: ICS Press, 1995), p. 405.

3. Kenneth Carlson et al., *American Prisons and Jails*. Vol. 2, *Population Trends and Projections* (Washington, D.C.: National Institute of Justice and Abt Associates, 1980).

4. Ibid.

5. Ibid.

6. Zimring and Hawkins, *The Scale of Imprisonment*, p. 78.

7. Nils Christie, *Crime as Industry* (Oslo, Norway: Universitetflag, 1993).

8. *USA Today*, March 13, 1996, p. A2.

9. *New York Times*, November 6, 1996, p. 1.

10. *USA Today*, March 13, 1996, p. A3.

11. Quoted in Bob Curley, "Corrections-Industrial Complex Feeds off War on Drugs," *Alcoholism and Drug Abuse Weekly* 7, No. 43 (November 6, 1995), p. 5.

12. U.S. Department of Justice, *Prisoners, 1991* (Washington, D.C.: Bureau of Justice Statistics, 1992).

13. U.S. Department of Justice, *Sourcebook of Criminal Justice Statistics, 1994* (Washington, D.C.: Bureau of Justice Statistics, 1995), p. 540.

14. Arnold Trebach and Eddy Engelsman. "Why Not Decriminalize?" *NPQ* [New Perspective Quarterly] (Summer 1989): 40–45.

15. National Institute on Drugs and Alcohol, *National Household Survey of Drug Abuse, Population Estimates, 1991* (Washington, D.C.: U.S. Government Printing Office, 1992).

16. On the Severity of U.S. penalties, see James Q. Wilson, *Thinking about Crime* (New York: Basic Books, 1975), p. xiv.

17. Herbert Jacob, *The Frustration of Policy: Responses to Crime by American Cities* (Boston: Little Brown, 1984), p. 162.

18. U.S. Department of Justice, *Setting Prison Terms* (Washington, D.C.: Bureau of Justice Statistics, August 1983), fig. 2.

19. *Rummel v. Estelle*, 445 U.S. 263 (1980).

20. Dianna Gordon, *The Justice Juggernaut* (New Brunswick, N.J.: Rutgers University Press, 1991), p. 22.

21. P. J. Langan, "America's Soaring Prison Population," *Science* 251 (March 1991): 1570.

22. Jacob, *The Frustration of Policy*, p. 160.

23. J. Livingston, *Crime and Criminology* (Englewood Cliffs, N.J.: Prentice-Hall, 1992), p. 543.

24. John F. Galliher, *Criminology: Human Rights, Criminal Law and Crime* (Englewood Cliffs, N.J: Prentice-Hall, 1989), p. 239.

25. Don C. Gibbons, *Society, Crime and Criminal Behavior*, 6th ed (Englewood Cliffs, N.J.: Prentice-Hall, 1992), p. 484.

26. Sheldon Rubin, *Psychiatry and Criminal Law* (Dobbs Ferry, N.Y.: Oceana Publications, 1965).

27. Charles Silberman, *Criminal Violence, Criminal Justice* (New York: Random House, 1978), p. 396.

28. P. J. Langan, "America's Soaring Prison Population," *Science* 251 (March 1991): 1570.

29. Gordon, *The Justice Juggernaut*, p. 5.

30. Joan Petersilia, "Alternatives to Prison—Cutting Cost and Crime," *Los Angeles Times*, January 31, 1988.

31. Norval Morris and Gordon Hawkins, *The Honest Politician's Guide to Crime Control* (Chicago: University of Chicago Press, 1970), p. 134.

32. U.S. Department of Justice, *Sourcebook of Criminal Justice Statistics, 1987* (Washington, D.C.: Bureau of Justice Statistics, 1988), p. 49.

33. U.S. Department of Justice, *Sourcebook of Criminal Justice Statistics* (Washington, D.C.: Bureau of Justice Statistics, 1992), p. 589.

34. Langan, "America's Soaring Prison Population," p. 1569.

35. U.S. Department of Justice, *Sourcebook of Criminal Justice Statistics, 1987*, p. 47.

36. U.S. Department of Justice, *Sourcebook of Criminal Justice Statistics, 1991*, p. 694.

37. Langan, "America's Soaring Prison Population," p. 1568

38. James Austin, "America's Growing Correctional-Industrial Complex," *National Council on Crime and Delinquency Focus Series* (San Francisco: National Council on Crime and Delinquency, 1990), pp. 1–7.

39. Franklin E. Zimring and Gordon Hawkins, *Prison Population and Criminal Justice Policy in California* (Berkeley, Calif.: Institute of Governmental Studies Press, 1992), p. 66.

40. Marcia Chambers, "As The Judges See It, They Are Unwilling Participants in a Futile and Unjust System," *National Law Journal* 15, No. 40 (June 7, 1993): 13–14.

41. Todd R. Clear and Anthony A. Braga, "Community Corrections," in James Q. Wilson and Joan Petersilia, eds., *Crime* (San Francisco: ICS Press, 1995), p. 421.

42. Todd R. Clear, *Harm in American Penology: Offenders, Victims and Their Communities* (Albany: State University of New York Press, 1994), p. 186.

43. Wayne LaFave, *Arrest: The Decision to Take a Person into Custody* (Boston: Little, Brown, 1965).

44. Alfred Blumstein, "Prisons," in James Q. Wilson and Joan Petersilia, eds., *Crime* (San Francisco: ICS Press, 1995), p. 397.

45. Zimring and Hawkins, *Prison Population and Criminal Justice Policy in California*, p. 65.

46. Ibid.

47. Blumstein, "Prisons," p. 418.

48. Zimring and Hawkins, *The Scale of Imprisonment*, p. 114.

49. Bill Krueger, "The Governor Left Out in the Cold," *Raleigh News and Observer*, December 26, 1992.

50. Van Denton, "Compromise Could Fuel Prison Building Boom," *News and Observer*, July 2, 1990.

51. Levona Page, "Chains on the Governor," *Columbia (South Carolina) State*, May 19, 1991.

52. Ibid.

53. Ibid.

54. Quoted in Sid Gaulden, "Quarter of Mothers Used Drugs, Alcohol," *Charleston News and Courier*, October 24, 1991.

55. Quoted in Cindi Ross Scoppe, "Campbell OKs Tighter Drug Law," *Columbia State*, June 26, 1990.

7

The Social Value of Prison Expansion

A study on the reasons for the variation in the increases in the rate of imprisonment among the fifty states inevitably raises the question of the effect on future crime rates of increasing imprisonment rates. While my task here has been to examine the causes for the marked differences among the different states regarding the investment of tax dollars in prisons, it seems appropriate to at least briefly examine the research on what social benefits are yielded by that investment. Does having more prisons lower crime rates? What is the experience in other nations? What does the research conclude about the costs and benefits of prisons?

WHY IMPRISONMENT RATES VARY OVER TIME AND FROM PLACE TO PLACE

Some observers have traced much of the growth in prisons in the United States to a growing crisis in authority that confronted the nation in the 1960s. They argue that "diminished confidence by voters in the nations' leaders created a threat to some politicians and an opportunity for others who could convince voters that they were capable of re-establishing the moral order."[1] A law-and-order political theme seemed to promise the voters a return to the "old days" of social stability and safe streets.

In 1973, even before the campaign for law and order got underway, conservative social critic James Q. Wilson wrote: "The United States has, on the whole, the most severe set of criminal penalties in its lawbooks of any advanced Western nation."[2] Nonetheless, the punitive sentencing policies in the United States became drastically more so during the next two decades.

By 1985, forty-six of the fifty states reported rates of imprisonment that were the highest that they had experienced in a century.[3] However, the most dramatic increases would come after 1985. The bottom line is this: in 1973 there were about 325,000 people behind bars for criminal offenses in the jails and prisons of United States; in 1996, there were more than 1.6 million people behind bars.

The incarceration rate (538 per 100,000 population) in the United States today is unmatched anywhere in the Western world. However, when we compare punishment for violent crime, incarceration rates are relatively similar in the United States and the other Organization for Economic Co-operation and Development (OECD) nations. Homicide, assault, robbery and rape receive relatively similar treatment in all Western democracies.[4]

It is when we come to punishing property offenses that a real gap is apparent. Perhaps even more significant is the fact that when we compare incarceration rates between the United States and the other OECD nations, it becomes clear that as the type of property crime being compared becomes less severe (i.e., lower amounts stolen) the disparity in punishments between the United States and other common-law nations increases, both with respect to the propensity to incarcerate and the length of time served.[5]

Most important, however, is the fact that the dramatic changes in sentencing patterns observed in the United States during the last two decades do not parallel the sentencing trends in other Western nations.[6] Despite similarities in patterns of crime rates, no other OECD nation saw anything like the prison expansion in the United States. The figures clearly demonstrate that only the United States had what could be called an explosion of imprisonment during this time, and that the explosion happened very unevenly among the fifty states.

Comparing American and European Crime Rates

Notwithstanding the widespread belief that the U.S. crime problem is unique in the world, the truth is that the nation's uniqueness is more apparent than real. The similarities in the rates of crime—other than homicide—among the OECD nations means that it is reasonable to compare the imprisonment policies in the United States with those of the other Western democracies.

In 1995, James Lynch, of American University and the Bureau of Social Science Research, wrote:

Newly available data on the prevalence of crime cross-nationally and some of the analyses of these data can make cross-national comparisons more useful in informing policy. First, these data indicate that the United States is not the most crime ridden of industrial democracies. The fact that the United States does not differ from other common law nations with respect to minor violence and serious property crime casts doubt on global indictments of the United States as having a criminal culture.[7]

In that same work, James Q. Wilson wrote that "any serious discussion of crime must begin with the fact that, except for homicide, most industrialized nations have crime rates that resemble those in the United States. All the world is coming to look like America."[8]

However, when it comes to prisons, nowhere else "looks like America."

Comparing American and European Imprisonment Rates

Emile Durkheim argued that the punishment of crime was an important social function because it reinforced social values and helped hold together society. He went on to suggest that if a society ever managed to eliminate very serious offenses, it would turn to less serious offenses to punish. It was the process of punishment—"the degradation ceremonies"—that gave the individual a sense of shared values.[9]

It just might be that today's U.S. citizenry is willing to punish less serious offenses out of the frustration felt by its inability to eliminate the more serious ones. The failure to deal successfully with persistently high homicide rates may be causing us to lash out vehemently at drug users and car thieves. Public attitudes toward further punitiveness seem to be an outgrowth of some irrational, moral panic. In the words of Zimring and Hawkins, "As long as there is a crime rate, one can consider the public demand for additional [prison] capacity to be unlimited."[10]

The human species apparently includes within it a small percentage of sociopaths and predators who victimize others, frequently in a compulsive and uncontrollable manner, which they themselves may not understand. No one would disagree that these individuals must be restrained in some fashion. Consequently, the argument against prisons is really an argument against the excessive use of prisons. Moreover, when a society more than quadruples the proportion of its population that is incarcerated in a two-decade period, that argument needs to be reexamined.

The imprisonment rate in other Western democracies helps to give some perspective to the U.S. rates. As Lynch concluded, "The U.S. has the highest per capita rates of incarceration of any industrialized democracy."[11] Other cross-cultural studies of crime show that "overall victimization rates in the United States are nearly identical to those in Canada, Australia and the Netherlands. Yet our incarceration rates are four times that of Canada, nearly six times that of Australia, and an astonishing ten times that of the Netherlands."[12]

Criminologists Michael Tonry has asked: "Why is the U.S. government, alone among the governments of the major English-speaking countries, claiming that harsh law-and-order policies will decrease crime rates?"[13] The question raised in this chapter is why that belief is so asymmetrically distributed among neighboring states.

There is a difference in the patterns of imprisonment use that is worth noting. As Lynch explained: "Prison use in the United States is not radically different from that in other industrialized nations for serious violence; but the propensity to incarcerate and time served in the United States is greater than in other nations for property and drug offenses."[14] In other words, when it comes to "petty offenses," the U.S. propensity for punishments that are Draconian by European standards increases dramatically. Moreover, there is evidence that this situation has eluded public perception.

It would appear that the U.S. public is largely unaware how many "petty offenders" are being held in the nation's prisons. A recent study on the seriousness of the crimes for which prison inmates are serving time in the United States is informative. As part of the study, a poll was taken, called "National Estimate of the Severity of Crimes Committed by Persons Admitted to State and Federal Prisons." The poll was done to determine what kinds of crimes the respondents considered to be "very serious crimes," "serious crimes," "moderate crimes" and "petty crimes." The researchers then compared the respondents' characterization of crimes to the offenses for which the nation's inmates were imprisoned. They found that 52 percent of inmates were serving time for what the poll indicated were considered "petty crimes"; 29 percent were imprisoned for "moderate crimes"; and only 14 percent for "serious crimes" and 4 percent for "very serious crimes."[15]

And why would the public not be confused when the advocates of more prisons seem to deliberately mislead them? Consider, for instance, Princeton University criminologist John DiIulio's argument against extending alternative programs for convicted offenders. In his widely acclaimed work, *No Escape: The Future of American Corrections*, DiIulio states that "95 percent of prisoners are violent offenders, repeat offenders (having two or more felony convictions), or violent repeat offenders; under 5 percent of prisoners can be meaningfully characterized as minor, petty or low-risk offenders."[16]

His statement leaves the impression that the vast majority of inmates are dangerous, violent criminals who should not be dealt with outside prison walls. This claim has been widely repeated in the media and in academia, and it deserves better scrutiny.

The Bureau of Justice statistics at the U.S. Department of Justice reports that for every one hundred individuals admitted to state prisons annually, only around 27 percent have been convicted of a violent offense.[17] The others are made up of property offenders (34 percent), drug offenders (29 percent) and public order offenses (7 percent).[18] How can we square these figures with what DiIulio claims?

The truth is that almost everyone who goes to prison is a "repeat offender" who is not necessarily also "violent." Almost no one goes to *prison* for their first offense. If you think about it, that 5 percent who are non-violent *and* non-repeat offenders must have stolen an enormous amount of money or sold an enormous amount of drugs in order to get a *prison* sentence for their first offense. When DiIulio says 95 percent are "violent or repeat" offenders, he fails to mention the fact that almost all first-time felony convictions for property or drug offenses result in either probation or a *jail* sentence of a year or less. They do not ordinarilly draw a *prison* sentence which, by definition, must involve a term of more than a year.

Of course, murderers and rapists will usually draw first offense *prison* terms but, taken together, they make up only about 1 percent of all offenders. In other words, the vast majority of people sent to prison have more than one felony conviction, that is, they are "repeat" offenders, but that in no way implies that they are "violent." They may have stolen a car years ago and received probation or sold marijuana and received a short jail term. But that makes them "repeat" offenders, as DiIulio points out. However, the impression he leaves with his readers is that they are also violent.

Arguing that 95 percent are a "violent or repeat" offender is like arguing that they are a "violent or right-handed" offender. It is very misleading.

DiIulio notwithstanding, the United States imprisons an extraordinary number of non-violent offenders and the public is, by and large, unaware of the extent to which their tax dollars are being used to incarcerate non-violent prisoners.

Twenty years ago, prison advocate James Q. Wilson argued the case for more prison construction on the ground that "since society clearly wishes its criminal laws more effectively enforced . . . this means rising prison populations perhaps for a long period."[19] It is unlikely that there has ever been a period when society did not want to have "its criminal laws more effectively enforced." However, with an estimated 40 million users of illegal drugs in the United States, imprisonment is clearly not the answer to the "effective enforcement of criminal laws." Moreover, the United States is the only nation that is trying to imprison away its drug problem. Prisons elsewhere are more likely to be reserved for serious predators.

THE SOCIAL VALUE OF IMPRISONMENT

The social value of imprisonment is a subject that very often provokes strong opinions that are based on robust, ardent intuition but little information. As Blumstein pointed out, "there remains a controversy between those who contend that prison makes criminals better and those who believe it makes them worse."[20] It should be borne in mind that this dispute is far from resolved.

The political ideology of the debate over prison usage runs along well-defined fault lines. Most simply put: "In the ideological division [that] is pervasive in the field of crime control, conservatives favor the construction of more prisons while liberals favor policies designed to reduce the number of prisons."[21] President Bush's attorney general succinctly stated one side of the argument when he said, "The choice is clear, more prison space or more crime."[22]

Given the exorbitant cost of running prisons in the United States (as much as $40 billion a year), how is it possible that economists have not provided a cost-benefit analysis of imprisonment? Recent years have seen some efforts in this direction. "Only in the last two decades," wrote one authority on imprisonment," has serious attention been paid by economists and other scholars to questions regarding . . . the cost-effectiveness of punishments."[23] Gary Becker explained this neglect among fellow economists as attributable to the fact that crime was "too immoral to merit any scientific attention."[24] However, with the growing political strength of the "correctional-industrial complex," perhaps the time has come for more attention to this area.

Arguments in Favor of Prisons

There are differences of opinion among criminologists about the social value of imprisonment. The Hobbesian view of human nature taken by some criminologists leads them inevitably to conclude that severe punishment is the only thing that will decrease crime; however, others argue that the threat of imprisonment has a minimal impact on criminal behavior and that imprisonment itself may actually increase the likelihood of future criminality in the released offender.

Traditionally, criminologists have explained the social benefits of imprisonment in four general areas: revenge for the victim, rehabilitation of the offender, deterrence of future criminal behavior by the offender and others, and the incapacitation of the offender during the time of imprisonment. The research into these areas has become far too extensive to do anything more than briefly summarize it here.

Revenge has a social value that is better debated by philosophers than by public policy analysts. It may be that the "degradation ceremonies" of which Durkheim wrote actually do have some effect in strengthening a sense of shared values, but this benefit to society is too nebulous to try to calculate in our analysis.

Rehabilitation has a long and irregular history. The numerous attempts at prisoner rehabilitation are over two centuries old in the United States, with little consensus on what works. In recent decades there has been little public belief in the ability of any professionals to force fundamental behavioral change on an unwilling offender. Some have argued that "the loss of confidence in rehabilitation has contributed significantly to the growth in prison populations."[25]

There are today few experts in the field who would argue that the social value of prison lies in either revenge or rehabilitation. Most often today, prison advocates argue that imprisonment can bring down crime rates in two ways: first the threat of punishment is thought to "deter" potential offenders; and second, the holding of inmates "incapacitates" the individuals from victimizing society for the period of imprisonment.

Deterrence is ordinarily discussed in terms of "specific deterrence" and "general deterrence." The former refers to the influence that punishment will have on a specific individual's future behavior; the latter refers to the influence that the punishment will have on the rest of the community. No one knows how much of a deterrent or incapacitative effect imprisonment actually has, but the most prominent arguments will be considered.

Arguments against Prisons

In 1996, Michael Tonry examined the research on the deterrent effect of prisons around the world. His conclusion was: "On the real-world question of whether increases in penalties significantly reduce the incidence of serious crimes, the consensus conclusion of governmental advisory bodies in many countries is maybe, a little, at most, but probably not."[26] This was consistent with the conclusions of the most exhaustive examination of the question of the deterrent effect ever done. In 1978, the National Academy of Sciences concluded: "In summary, we cannot assert that the evidence warrants an affirmative conclusion regarding deterrence."[27] However, there are other opinions about deterrence that should be considered.

Charles Murray, for instance, conducted a study in 1986 that concluded that incarcerating juvenile offenders would reduce the rate at which they engaged in crime.[28] Moreover, a few other researchers found that where punishment is severe and certain, crime rates tend to be lower than where it is less severe and less certain.[29]

Nonetheless, a major review of deterrence research concluded that no connection could be demonstrated between imprisonment and increases or decreases in crime.[30] Some others found that the effect on crime rates of increasing imprisonment is minuscule.[31] After examining all the current research in this area, Livingston concluded, "My own conclusion is that prison is not much of a specific deterrent."[32] Moreover, some have suggested that higher imprisonment rates may actually increase overall crime rates by making those incarcerated even more of a threat to society on their release.[33] In the aggregate, the argument goes, a million parolees from prison are, in the long run, more likely to commit additional offenses than a million comparable offenders who served their time on probation and thereby avoided the harmful influence of prison life.

A third perspective on this question is that we just do not know whether higher imprisonment rates will result in lower crime rates.[34] In a study that stretched over thirty years, Herbert Jacob and his colleagues concluded that despite extensive research on the subject, a direct link between increased imprisonment and lower crime rates has never been empirically established.[35]

The well-respected study by Isaac Erhlich[36] concluded that at best we could expect a 5 percent increase in the crime rate if every inmate's sentence were suddenly cut in half. If decreasing the amount of time served by the average inmate would have only a minor impact on crime rates, what would the effect be of increasing the number of inmates in prison?

Another study on deterrence looked at the possible effects of massive increases in imprisonment—that is, the opposite side of the coin from Erhlich. Greenwood and Abrahamse studied the possible repercussions of increasing the prison population by 50 percent and concluded that such a move would not have more than a minor effect on crime and could reduce the crime rate by no more than 4 percent.[37]

In an exhaustive review of the existing research on deterrence and incapacitation, Elliott Currie concluded, "The limits of imprisonment to reduce crime are understood in principle by most serious criminologists, of whatever ideological stripe." He argued that criminologists, whether on the left, right, or center, "generally acknowledge that only a fraction of serious crime can be prevented by increased imprisonment."[38]

If Currie is right, then why do researchers like Murray and Gibbs argue that imprisonment can reduce crime? Currie concluded that "those who argue for more rigorous efforts at deterrence and incapacitation through harsher sentences and more prison cells base that argument on the premise that there is little else we can do that will have much effect on crime."[39] He did not address the political benefits of advocating harsher sentences.

Despite the fact that the literature on the value of imprisonment has grown substantially in recent years, there remains fundamental disagreement among scholars about the benefits of increasing the rate of imprisonment. The recent decrease in the rate of reported crime in the United States, coming as it has at a time when the rate of imprisonment is at an all-time high, has caused many to assume that the former was caused by the latter.

It may be that the drugs that are not sold by incarcerated drug dealers will be sold anyway by those who took their places after their arrests. However, at the very least, incarcerated car thieves cannot steal cars until after their release, and if enough car thieves are imprisoned, then the rate of car theft must fall. However, will the paroled car thieves pose a greater danger of more serious offenses than had they not been caught? The truth is that no one knows.

Imprisonment Increases and Falling Crime Rates in the 1990s

The suggestion that the massive increases in incarceration during the 1980s and 1990s may be responsible for the encouraging crime statistics of the 1990s is worth addressing. Both the FBI's *Uniform Crime Reports* and the National Crime Survey show lower crime rates in 1995 than they did in 1980. One argument suggests that, notwithstanding the fact that demographers had predicted this decrease as the baby boomers aged out of the crime-prone age group, the real reason for the decrease is the deterrent and incapacitative effect of increasing imprisonment. What does the research of the 1990s conclude about this argument?

Criminologists James Austin and John Irwin compared crime and imprisonment rates in 1991 in each state during the 1980s and found no firm correlation. South Dakota's imprisonment rate was twice that of neighboring North Dakota, for example, but crime in both states rose and fell at roughly the same rates.[40] More important, the reported crime rate in South Dakota was not much different from that of North Dakota. Where, then, is the relationship between imprisonment rates and crime rates?

Scholars like Alfred Blumstein of Carnegie-Mellon have spent their entire careers studying the social impact of prisons, often with great frustration. In 1995, Blumstein pointed out, "There has been a massive growth in the prison populations between the mid-1970s and the mid-1990s, with no demonstrated strong effect on crime rates."[41]

In an extensive study of the recent crime and imprisonment data nationwide, one scholar concluded, "Punishment has increased inexorably over the last two decades, but it must be fully faced that from year to year, crime rates have sometimes increased, sometimes decreased, and sometimes have not changed much."[42]

One of the most respected scholars in the field, Norval Morris, reviewed the Zimring and Hawkins 1992 study of prison growth in California and called it a "devastating refutation of the prison-building path . . . accepted by those whose simple view is that crime can be imprisoned away."[43]

Yet another researcher in the field, using 1995 statistics, tried in vain to find a connection between changes in crime rates and changes in imprisonment rates and concluded that "increases in incarceration rates were not driven by comparable increases in crime."[44] Echoing Blumstein's conclusion in one of the most comprehensive study on imprisonment use in the United States, Todd Clear would conclude: "The argument that punishment changes produce crime changes is not supported by these data. . . . The increase in punishment did not produce a commensurate reduction in the amount of crime."[45]

Even James Q. Wilson—the most well-known advocate of prison expansion through the 1970s and 1980s—conceded in 1995: "Very large increases in the prison population can produce only modest reductions in crime rates. Doubling the prison population probably produces only a 10 to 20 percent reduction in the crime rate."[46] Wilson also dismissed the argument that the recent explosion in prison population resulted in the reduction in crime. "It would be foolhardy" wrote Wilson and Joan Petersilia in 1995, "to explain the drop in the crime rate by the rise in imprisonment rates."[47] Even John DiIulio, a Princeton criminologist who is often quoted for his support of increasing punitiveness, has written that the liberal argument that "prisons don't pay" is probably closer to the truth than the conservative argument that they do.[48]

The National Academy of Science's Panel on Understanding and Control of Violent Behavior in 1993 asked about the effect of increasing the prison population on violent crime and answered, "[A]pparently very little."[49] In his 1996 work, *Sentencing Matters*, Michael Tonry pointed out that this panel was initiated at the request of Ronald Reagan's Department of Justice and funded by both the Reagan and Bush administrations. He concluded that this fact was not "irrelevant" and that this panel was "an establishmentarian body bearing the imprimatur of Conservative Republican administrations."[50]

My own research on the question of the association between increases in crime rates and the increases in imprisonment rates showed a low correlational coefficient, but will the states that increased imprisonment significantly over a twenty-year period experience lower rates of crime increase than the states that did not? In order to test this question, I divided the fifty states into the twenty-five that increased their imprisonment rates less than the median increase (an average of 181 percent) and the twenty-five that increased at a rate above the median (average of 368 percent). Consider Tables 6.1 and 6.2 from the previous chapter. The high-increase states, which invested in more prisons, actually show less increase in crime than the low-increase states over the twenty years between 1972 and 1992.

However, the numbers offer little solace to those who would suggest prison as a way of significantly impacting crime. A cost-benefit analysis of these figures suggests the futility of imprisonment as a means of addressing the crime problem. While increasing their imprisonment rates by an average of 368 percent between 1972 and 1992, the high-increase states managed to keep the increase in the reported crime rate down to an average 46 percent. At the same time, the low-increase states increased their imprisonment rates by just an average of 181 percent and saw their reported crime rate increase by an average 52 percent.

If the low-increase states had followed the same policies as the high-increase states and increased their imprisonment rate by 368 percent instead of 181 percent, they would have imprisoned approximately 189,000 more offenders than they in fact did. In other words, if just twenty-five states had increased their number of prisoners by an additional 189,000 inmates (about as many as all the prison inmates nationwide in 1972), then perhaps we could have expected that the reported crime rate in those twenty-five states would have grown at approximately 46 percent instead of 52 percent. That, of course, is true only if we assume that the increase in reported crime was attributable solely to factors that would have been removed by increased imprisonment.

In today's dollars, the cost of the additional 189,000 inmates would be close to $5 billion per year, enough to hire and pay around 125,000 police officers. As only 27 percent of all prison admissions last year were for violent offenses, a cost-benefit analysis of further prison expansion should compare the relative benefits to society of spending more tax dollars on more prisons versus increasing police protection. There is probably a maximum number of tax dollars that voters are willing to spend on criminal justice. Clearly, priorities should be reassessed concerning the dollars spent on police and those spent on prisons.

CONCLUSION

This work has explored the reason for the rapid expansion of the prisons in the United States between 1972 and 1992. That expansion averaged over 250 percent in the fifty states during this two-decade period, but there were marked variations in the rates of growth in different states.

The three leading theories dealing with prison growth did not offer very satisfying explanations for the contemporary prison expansion. The Blumstein-Durkheim theory, the Marxist-based Rusche-Kirchheimer theory, and the racial bias theory were all examined to evaluate their relative explanatory strength.

The intuitive association of rising crime rates and rising rates of imprisonment was examined in Chapter 3. Social control theorists, such as Alfred Blumstein, claimed to find support in Durkheimian theory and argued that prisons would grow as a natural reaction to growing crime rates. However, when Blumstein himself looked at the data on imprisonment expansion during the recent past, he reconsidered, and largely rejected, his earlier findings. This awakened my interest in the association between crime and imprisonment rates.

Other researchers in this field had already concluded that the association of increases in the rate of crime and the rate of imprisonment was small. However, their research was aggregated on a national level and none of the research in this area included a bivariate correlation of the increases in the crime rate and the increases in the imprisonment rate on the state level. When the data was disaggregated to a state level to see if the variations in the increase in crime were associated with the variations in the imprisonment rates of each state, the coefficient of correlation remained low enough to be considered, at best, just a partial explanation of prison expansion.

The crime most likely to result in a prison sentence is homicide. In 1992, the rate of homicide varied from a low of 1.6 per 100,000 in Maine to a high of 20.3 per 100,000 in Louisiana. Despite this fact, the correlation coefficient for homicide rates (HOM92 in Appendix 5) and increases in imprisonment rates (PRISINCP in Appendix 5) was just .0567, with a p of .696. Clearly, something other than high homicide rates was responsible for the variation in the growth of imprisonment rates.

The Marxist theory of Rusche-Kircheimer suggests that prison growth is an outgrowth of economic conditions. However, the correlational coefficients between the growth of the imprisonment rate in a state and economic conditions in that state did not reveal a very strong association between the two. Correlating the growth of the rate of imprisonment (VAR 1 in Appendix 6) with the proportion of the population living below the poverty level (VAR 9) yielded a coefficient of $-.1400$, with a p of .332; the correlation coefficient for the prison expansion rate and the unemployment rate (VAR 10) was .19, with a p of .172. However, when it came to the correlation between the average income in a state (VAR 8) and their rate of imprisonment growth, the coefficient was higher than for any of the other variables, namely .2841, with a p of .046. While still not a very strong association, it may suggest that prisons are a luxury that can only be indulged by wealthier states.

The race bias theory, most recently espoused by Michael Tonry, was also examined. Tonry suggested that patterns of drug selling in ghetto areas were such as to make blacks an easy target for police arrests. Therefore, argued Tonry, the war on drugs would inevitably result in a massive increase of blacks going to prison. When the growth of the imprisonment rate in the fifty states was correlated with both the percentage of the population in that state that was African-American and the rate of drug arrests per 100,000, the association was again very weak. The correlation between the growth of imprisonment rates and the percent of the population that was black was just .07. Moreover, the correlation between the drug arrest rate and the growth of imprisonment was even lower (.06). While Tonry's theory does seem, on its face, to have logical merit, and while the proportion of inmates being admitted to prisons that are either black or drug offenders has grown quickly, the low correlations suggest that imprisonment expansion is not associated with a high rate of drug arrests or a large African-American population.

These findings left largely unanswered the original question: Why did some states increase the imprisonment rate so much more rapidly than others? Over the two decades, the variation in the rate of increase in imprisonment from the highest to the lowest state was thirteen to one. Certainly some of this variation can be explained by the socioeconomic variables we have examined, but there must be other factors at work. It is my conclusion that a major factor was the law-and-order politics of governors in various states.

Seven law-and-order governors were identified based on the rate of increase in imprisonment during their administration. Their views on crime and punishment were analyzed and compared to those of their counterparts in contiguous states. The evidence gathered suggests that where a state elected an advocate of punitive policies concerning crime, there was a rapid increase in the rate of imprisonment without regard to changes in the crime rate. In contiguous states where governors advocated less punitive policies, however, the rate of imprisonment did not expand.

Moreover, I found evidence that the expansion came through both formal and informal processes and, moreover, that the informal processes may actually play a more significant role. When an individual who advocates a strong "tough on crime" policy is elected governor, the informal message sent to the street-level bureaucrats of the criminal justice system can have an immediate effect on prison expansion.

The continuation of the kind of prison expansion that has been seen in the recent past would appear to be very probable. Advocacy of further prison growth appears to be winning more bipartisan support as Democrats learn the political popularity of law-and-order platforms. (All but one of the seven "law and order" governors studied here were Republicans.) Prison construction programs in 1996 are bigger than ever, and three strikes laws appear to be growing in popularity.

The cost of prison expansion in terms of broken families and lost opportunities for education or job training is difficult to measure. The moral or emotional damage done to the individual incarcerated in penal institutions cannot be measured. However, the cost of keeping an inmate in prison and the cost of building that cell can be measured, and the cost has increased in the United States to a point where the dubious benefits of further imprisonment expansion should be reconsidered.

Herbert Jacob, in looking at what he called "the politics of prison expansion" claimed that this is something about which "we know very little, in large part because it has long been ignored both by political scientists and by criminologists specializing in corrections."[51] Jacob concluded that there had never been a study on such things as "the election of a law and order state government" and its influence on prison population.[52] Hopefully, the analysis of the politics of these seven law-and-order governors will offer a beginning to such a study.

NOTES

1. Francis T. Cullen, Gregory A. Clark, and John F. Wozniak, "Explaining the Get Tough Movement: Can the Public Be Blamed?" *Federal Probation* 49 (1985): 17.

2. James Q. Wilson, *Thinking about Crime* (New York: Basic Books, 1975), p. xiv.

3. Franklin E. Zimring and Gordon Hawkins, *The Scale of Imprisonment* (Chicago: University of Chicago Press, 1991), p. 152.

4. James Lynch, "Crime in International Perspective," in James Q. Wilson and Joan Petersilia, eds., *Crime* (San Francisco: ICS Press, 1995), p. 33.

5. Ibid., p. 37.

6. Zimring and Hawkins, *The Scale of Imprisonment*, p. 119.

7. Lynch, "Crime in International Perspective," p. 36.

8. Wilson, *Thinking about Crime*, p. 489.

9. Sue Titus Reid, *Crime and Criminology* (Madison: Brown and Benchmark Publishers, 1996), p. 143.

10. Zimring and Hawkins, *The Scale of Imprisonment*, p. 79.

11. Lynch, "Crime in International Perspective," p. 36.

12. Jan van Dijk, Pat Mayhew, and Martin Killias, *Experiences of Crime across the World* (Boston: Kluwer, 1990).

13. Michael Tonry, *Malign Neglect* (New York: Oxford University Press, 1995), p. 79.

14. Lynch, "Crime in International Perspective," p. 11.

15. Quoted in James Austin and John Irwin, *Who Goes To Prison?* (San Francisco: National Council on Crime and Delinquency, 1991).

16. John DiIulio, Jr., *No Escape: The Future of American Corrections* (New York: Basic Books, 1991), p. 4.

17. U.S. Department of Justice, *National Corrections Reporting Program, 1992* (Washington, D.C.: Bureau of Justice Statistics, 1994), p. 13.

18. Ibid.

19. James Q. Wilson, *Thinking About Crime* (New York: Basic Books, 1975), p. 173.

20. Alfred Blumstein, "Prisons," in James Q. Wilson and Joan Petersilia, eds., *Crime* (San Francisco: ICS Press, 1995), p. 396.

21. Zimring and Hawkins, *The Scale of Imprisonment*, p. 206.

22. William P. Barr, "Speech to California's District Attorney's Association," *Federal Sentencing Reporter* 4, no. 6 (1990): 345.

23. Zimring and Hawkins, *The Scale of Imprisonment*, p. 91.

24. Gary S. Becker, "Crime and Punishment: An Economic Approach," *Journal of Political Economy* 76 (1968): 169–217.

25. Blumstein, "Prisons," p. 396. See also Robert Martinson, "What Works? Questions and Answers About Prison Reform," *The Public Interest* 35 (1974): 22–54.

26. Michael Tonry, *Sentencing Matters* (New York: Oxford University Press, 1996), p. 137.

27. Alfred Blumstein, J. Cohen, and D. Nagin, *Deterrence and Incapacitation: Estimating the Effects of Criminal Sanctions on Crime Rates* (Washington, D.C.: National Academy of Sciences, 1978), p. 42–44.

28. Quoted in Charles Murray and Louis A. Cox, *Beyond Probation: Juvenile Corrections and the Chronic Offender* (Beverley Hills, Calif.: Sage Publications, 1986).

29. Blumstein, Cohen, and Nagin, *Deterrence and Incapacitation*, pp. 42–44.

30. Philip Cook, "Research in Criminal Deterrence: Laying the Groundwork for the Second Decade," in Norval Morris and Michael Tonry, eds., *Crime and Justice:*

An Annual Review of Research, Vol. 2 (Chicago: University of Chicago Press, 1979), pp. 211–268.

31. Steven Clarke, "Getting Them Out of Circulation: Does Incapacitation of Juvenile Offenders Reduce Crime?" *Journal of Criminal Law and Criminology* 65 (1974): 528–535; Charles Silberman, *Criminal Violence, Criminal Justice* (New York: Random House, 1978), p. 191; Franklin E. Zimring and Gordon J. Hawkins, *Deterrence* (Chicago: University of Chicago Press, 1973); Dianna Gordon, *The Justice Juggernaut* (New Brunswick, N.J.: Rutgers University Press, 1991), p. 214; Stephen Van Dine, John Conrad, and Simon Dinitz, *Restraining the Wicked* (Lexington, Mass.: Lexington Books, 1979), p. 123.

32. Jay Livingston, *Crime and Criminology* (Englewood Cliffs, N.J.: Prentice-Hall, 1992), p. 548.

33. Elliot Currie, *Confronting Crime: An American Challenge* (New York: Pantheon Books, 1985), p. 75.

34. Norval Morris and Gordon Hawkins, *The Honest Politician's Guide to Crime Control* (Chicago: University of Chicago Press, 1970), p. 261.

35. Herbert Jacob, *The Frustration of Policy: Responses to Crime by American Cities* (Boston: Little, Brown, 1984), p. 162.

36. Isaac Erhlich, "Participation in Illegitimate Activities: An Economic Analysis," in C. S. Becer and W. M. Landes, eds., *Essays in the Economics of Crime and Punishment* (New York: National Bureau of Economic Research, 1974).

37. Peter Greenwood and Allan Abrahamse, *Selective Incapacitation* (Santa Monica, Calif.: Rand Corporation, 1982), p. 541.

38. Currie, *Confronting Crime*, p. 52.

39. Ibid., p. 100.

40. James Austin and John Irwin, *Who Goes To Prison?* (San Francisco: National Council on Crime and Delinquency, 1991).

41. Blumstein, "Prisons," p. 416.

42. Todd T. Clear, *Harm in American Penology: Offenders, Victims and Their Communities* (Albany: State University of New York Press, 1994), p. 75.

43. Quoted in Franklin E. Zimring and Gordon Hawkins, *Prison Population and Criminal Justice Policy in California* (Berkeley Calif.: Institute of Governmental Studies Press, 1992), p. ix.

44. Wayne N. Welsh, "Jail Overcrowding and Court Ordered Reform," in Roslyn Muraskin and Albert R. Roberts, eds., *Visions for Change: Crime and Justice in the Twenty-first Century* (Upper Saddle River, N.J.: Prentice-Hall, 1996), p. 202.

45. Clear, *Harm in American Penology*, p. 63.

46. James Q. Wilson, *Thinking about Crime* (New York: Basic Books, 1975), p. xiv.

47. James Q. Wilson and Joan Petersilia, eds., *Crime* (San Francisco: ICS Press, 1995), p. 490.

48. Quoted in John J. DiIulio and Anne M. Diehl, "Does Prison Pay?" (Princeton University Center of Domestic and Comparative Policy Studies, unpublished manuscript).

49. Albert J. Reiss and Jeffrey Roth, eds., *Understanding and Controlling Violence* (Washington, D.C.: National Academy Press, 1993).

50. Tonry, *Sentencing Matters*, p. 137.

51. Jacob, *The Frustration of Policy*, p. 209.

52. Ibid.

Appendixes

Appendix 1:
Uniform Crime Reports from 1960 to 1992

Estimated number and rate (per 100,000 inhabitants) of offenses known to police

By offense, United States, 1960-92

	Total Crime Index	Violent crime	Property crime	Murder and non-negligent manslaughter	Forcible rape	Robbery	Aggravated assault	Burglary	Larceny-theft	Motor vehicle theft
Number of offenses										
1960	3,384,200	288,460	3,095,700	9,110	17,190	107,840	154,320	912,100	1,855,400	328,200
1961	3,488,000	289,390	3,198,600	8,740	17,220	106,670	156,760	949,600	1,913,000	336,000
1962	3,752,200	301,510	3,450,700	8,530	17,550	110,860	164,570	994,300	2,089,600	366,800
1963	3,109,500	316,970	3,792,500	8,640	17,650	116,470	174,210	1,086,400	2,297,800	408,300
1964	4,564,600	364,220	4,200,400	9,360	21,420	130,390	203,050	1,213,200	2,514,400	472,800
1965	4,739,400	387,390	4,352,000	9,960	23,410	138,690	215,330	1,282,500	2,572,600	496,900
1966	5,223,500	430,180	4,793,300	11,040	25,820	157,990	235,330	1,410,100	2,822,000	561,200
1967	5,903,400	499,930	5,403,500	12,240	27,620	202,910	257,160	1,632,100	3,111,600	659,800
1968	6,720,200	595,010	6,125,200	13,800	31,670	262,840	286,700	1,858,900	3,482,700	783,600
1969	7,410,900	661,870	6,749,000	14,760	37,170	298,850	311,090	1,981,900	3,888,600	878,500
1970	8,098,000	738,820	7,359,200	16,000	37,990	349,860	334,970	2,205,000	4,225,800	928,400
1971	8,588,200	816,500	7,771,700	17,780	42,260	387,700	368,760	2,399,300	4,424,200	948,200
1972	8,248,800	834,900	7,413,900	18,670	46,850	376,290	393,090	2,375,500	4,151,200	887,200
1973	8,718,100	875,910	7,842,200	19,640	51,400	384,220	420,650	2,565,500	4,347,900	928,800
1974	10,253,400	974,720	9,278,700	20,710	55,400	442,400	456,210	3,039,200	5,262,500	977,100
1975	11,292,400	1,039,710	10,252,700	20,510	56,090	470,500	492,620	3,265,300	5,977,700	1,009,600
1976	11,349,700	1,004,210	10,345,500	18,780	57,080	427,810	500,530	3,108,700	6,270,800	966,000
1977	10,984,500	1,029,580	9,955,000	19,120	63,500	412,610	534,350	3,071,500	5,905,700	977,700
1978	11,209,000	1,085,550	10,123,400	19,560	67,610	426,930	571,460	3,128,300	5,991,000	1,004,100
1979	12,249,500	1,208,030	11,041,500	21,460	76,390	480,700	629,480	3,327,700	6,601,000	1,112,800
1980	13,408,300	1,344,520	12,063,700	23,040	82,990	565,840	672,650	3,795,200	7,136,900	1,131,700
1981	13,423,300	1,361,820	12,061,900	22,520	82,500	592,910	663,900	3,779,700	7,194,400	1,087,800
1982	12,974,400	1,322,390	11,652,000	21,010	78,770	553,130	669,480	3,447,100	7,142,500	1,062,400
1983	12,108,600	1,258,090	10,850,500	19,310	78,920	506,570	653,290	3,129,900	6,712,800	1,007,900
1984	11,881,800	1,273,280	10,608,500	18,960	84,230	485,010	685,350	2,984,400	6,591,900	1,032,200
1985	12,431,400	1,328,800	11,102,600	18,980	88,670	497,870	723,250	3,073,300	6,926,400	1,102,900
1986	13,211,900	1,489,170	11,722,700	20,610	91,460	542,780	834,320	3,241,400	7,257,200	1,224,100
1987	13,508,700	1,484,000	12,024,700	20,100	91,110	517,700	855,090	3,236,200	7,499,900	1,288,700
1988'	13,923,100	1,566,220	12,356,900	20,680	92,490	542,970	910,090	3,218,100	7,705,900	1,432,900
1989	14,251,400	1,646,040	12,605,400	21,500	94,500	578,330	951,710	3,168,200	7,872,400	1,564,800
1990	14,475,600	1,820,130	12,655,500	23,440	102,560	639,270	1,054,860	3,073,900	7,945,700	1,635,900
1991	14,872,900	1,911,770	12,961,100	24,700	106,590	687,730	1,092,740	3,157,200	8,142,200	1,661,700
1992	14,438,200	1,932,270	12,505,900	23,760	109,060	672,480	1,126,970	2,979,900	7,915,200	1,610,800

118

Rate per 100,000 inhabitants

Year										
1960	1,887.2	160.9	1,726.3	5.1	9.6	60.1	86.1	508.6	1,034.7	183.0
1961	1,906.1	158.1	1,747.9	4.8	9.4	58.3	85.7	518.9	1,045.4	183.6
1962	2,019.8	162.3	1,857.5	4.6	9.4	59.7	88.6	535.2	1,124.8	197.4
1963	2,180.3	168.2	2,012.1	4.6	9.4	61.8	92.4	576.4	1,219.1	216.6
1964	2,388.1	190.6	2,197.5	4.9	11.2	68.2	106.2	634.7	1,315.5	247.4
1965	2,449.0	200.2	2,248.8	5.1	12.1	71.7	111.3	662.7	1,329.3	256.8
1966	2,670.8	220.0	2,450.9	5.6	13.2	80.8	120.3	721.0	1,442.9	286.9
1967	2,989.7	253.2	2,736.5	6.2	14.0	102.8	130.2	826.6	1,575.8	334.1
1968	3,370.2	298.4	3,071.8	6.9	15.9	131.8	143.8	932.3	1,746.6	393.0
1969	3,680.0	328.7	3,351.3	7.3	18.5	148.4	154.5	984.1	1,930.9	436.2
1970	3,984.5	363.5	3,621.0	7.9	18.7	172.1	164.8	1,084.9	2,079.3	456.8
1971	4,164.7	396.0	3,768.8	8.6	20.5	188.0	178.8	1,163.5	2,145.5	459.8
1972	3,961.4	401.0	3,560.4	9.0	22.5	180.7	188.8	1,140.8	1,993.6	426.1
1973	4,154.4	417.4	3,737.0	9.4	24.5	183.1	200.5	1,222.5	2,071.9	442.6
1974	4,850.4	461.1	4,389.3	9.8	26.2	209.3	215.8	1,437.7	2,489.5	462.2
1975	5,298.5	487.8	4,810.7	9.6	26.3	220.8	231.1	1,532.1	2,804.8	473.7
1976	5,287.3	467.8	4,819.5	8.8	26.6	199.3	233.2	1,448.2	2,921.3	450.0
1977	5,077.6	475.9	4,601.7	8.8	29.4	190.7	240.0	1,419.8	2,729.9	451.9
1978	5,140.3	497.8	4,642.5	9.0	31.0	195.8	262.1	1,434.6	2,747.4	460.5
1979	5,565.5	548.9	5,016.6	9.7	34.7	218.4	286.0	1,511.9	2,999.1	505.6
1980	5,950.0	596.6	5,353.3	10.2	36.8	251.1	298.5	1,684.1	3,167.0	502.2
1981	5,858.2	594.3	5,263.9	9.8	36.0	258.7	289.7	1,649.5	3,139.7	474.7
1982	5,603.6	571.1	5,032.5	9.1	34.0	238.9	289.2	1,488.8	3,084.8	458.8
1983	5,175.0	537.7	4,637.4	8.3	33.7	216.5	279.2	1,337.7	2,868.9	430.8
1984	5,031.3	539.2	4,492.1	7.9	35.7	205.4	290.2	1,263.7	2,791.3	437.1
1985	5,207.1	556.6	4,650.5	7.9	37.1	208.5	302.9	1,287.3	2,901.2	462.0
1986	5,480.4	617.7	4,862.6	8.6	37.9	225.1	346.1	1,344.6	3,010.3	507.8
1987	5,550.0	609.7	4,940.3	8.3	37.4	212.7	351.3	1,329.6	3,081.3	529.4
1988	5,664.2	637.2	5,027.1	8.4	37.6	220.9	370.2	1,309.2	3,134.9	582.9
1989	5,741.0	663.7	5,077.9	8.7	38.1	233.0	383.4	1,276.3	3,171.3	630.4
1990	5,820.3	731.8	5,088.5	9.4	41.2	257.0	424.1	1,235.9	3,194.8	657.8
1991	5,897.8	758.1	5,139.7	9.8	42.3	272.7	433.3	1,252.0	3,228.8	659.0
1992	5,660.2	757.5	4,902.7	9.3	42.8	263.6	441.8	1,168.2	3,103.0	631.5

Appendix 2:
National Crime Victimization Survey
from 1973 to 1992

Estimated number and rate (per 1,000 units of each respective category) of personal and household victimizations

By type of victimization, United States, 1973-92

(Number of victimizations in thousands. Rates for personal crimes per 1,000 persons age 12 and older; rates for household crimes per 1,000 households.)

			Type of victimization											
	Personal crimes										Household crimes			
		Crimes of violence						Crimes of theft						
					Assault				Personal larceny		Total			Motor
	Total personal crimes	Total	Rape	Robbery	Total	Aggravated	Simple	Total	With contact	Without contact	household crimes	Burglary	Larceny	vehicle theft
Number of victimizations														
1973	20,322	5,351	156	1,108	4,087	1,655	2,432	14,971	504	14,466	15,340	6,459	7,537	1,344
1974	21,399	5,510	163	1,199	4,148	1,735	2,413	15,889	520	15,369	17,012	6,721	8,933	1,358
1975	21,867	5,573	154	1,147	4,272	1,631	2,641	16,294	524	15,770	17,400	6,744	9,223	1,433
1976	22,118	5,599	145	1,111	4,344	1,695	2,648	16,519	497	16,022	17,199	6,663	9,301	1,235
1977	22,835	5,902	154	1,083	4,664	1,738	2,926	16,933	461	16,472	17,480	6,765	9,418	1,297
1978	22,991	5,941	171	1,038	4,732	1,708	3,024	17,050	549	16,501	17,421	6,704	9,352	1,365
1979	22,541	6,159	192	1,116	4,851	1,769	3,082	16,382	511	15,871	18,708	6,685	10,630	1,393
1980	21,430	6,130	174	1,209	4,747	1,707	3,041	15,300	558	14,742	18,822	6,973	10,468	1,381
1981	22,445	6,582	178	1,381	5,024	1,796	3,228	15,863	605	15,258	19,009	7,394	10,176	1,439
1982	22,012	6,459	153	1,334	4,973	1,754	3,219	15,553	577	14,976	17,745	6,663	9,705	1,377
1983	20,560	5,903	154	1,149	4,600	1,517	3,083	14,657	563	14,095	16,441	6,063	9,114	1,264
1984	19,810	6,021	180	1,097	4,744	1,727	3,017	13,789	530	13,259	15,733	5,643	8,750	1,340
1985	19,297	5,823	138	985	4,699	1,605	3,094	13,474	523	12,951	15,567	5,594	8,703	1,270
1986	18,750	5,515	130	1,009	4,376	1,543	2,833	13,235	536	12,699	15,368	5,557	8,455	1,356
1987	19,371	5,796	148	1,046	4,602	1,587	3,014	13,575	509	13,066	15,966	5,705	8,788	1,473
1988	19,966	5,910	127	1,048	4,734	1,741	2,993	14,056	489	13,567	15,830	5,777	8,419	1,634
1989	19,690	5,861	135	1,092	4,634	1,665	2,969	13,829	543	13,287	16,127	5,352	8,955	1,820
1990	18,984	6,009	130	1,150	4,729	1,601	3,128	12,975	637	12,338	15,420	5,148	8,304	1,968
1991	19,472	6,587	174	1,203	5,210	1,634	3,575	12,885	497	12,389	16,025	5,187	8,702	2,136
1992	18,832	6,621	141	1,226	5,255	1,849	3,406	12,211	485	11,726	14,817	4,757	8,101	1,959

Rate													
1973	123.6	32.6	1.0	6.7	24.9	10.1	14.8	91.1	3.1	88.0	217.8	91.7	107.0	19.1
1974	128.1	33.0	1.0	7.2	24.8	10.4	14.4	95.1	3.1	92.0	235.7	93.1	123.8	18.8
1975	128.9	32.8	0.9	6.8	25.2	9.6	15.6	96.0	3.1	92.9	236.5	91.7	125.4	19.5
1976	128.7	32.6	0.8	6.5	25.3	9.9	15.4	96.1	2.9	93.2	229.5	88.9	124.1	16.5
1977	131.2	33.9	0.9	6.2	26.8	10.0	16.8	97.3	2.7	94.6	228.8	88.5	123.3	17.0
1978	130.5	33.7	1.0	5.9	26.9	9.7	17.2	96.8	3.1	93.6	223.4	86.0	119.9	17.5
1979	126.4	34.5	1.1	6.3	27.2	9.9	17.3	91.9	2.9	89.0	235.3	84.1	133.7	17.5
1980	116.3	33.3	0.9	6.6	25.8	9.3	16.5	83.0	3.0	80.0	227.4	84.3	126.5	16.7
1981	120.5	35.3	1.0	7.4	27.0	9.6	17.3	85.1	3.3	81.9	226.0	87.9	121.0	17.1
1982	116.8	34.3	0.8	7.1	26.4	9.3	17.1	82.5	3.1	79.5	208.2	78.2	113.9	16.2
1983	107.9	31.0	0.8	6.0	24.1	8.0	16.2	76.9	3.0	74.0	189.8	70.0	105.2	14.6
1984	103.2	31.4	0.9	5.7	24.7	9.0	15.7	71.8	2.8	69.1	178.7	64.1	99.4	15.2
1985	99.4	30.0	0.7	5.1	24.2	8.3	15.9	69.4	2.7	66.7	174.4	62.7	97.5	14.2
1986	95.6	28.1	0.7	5.1	22.3	7.9	14.4	67.5	2.7	64.7	170.0	61.5	93.5	15.0
1987	98.0	29.3	0.8	5.3	23.3	8.0	15.2	68.7	2.6	66.1	173.9	62.1	95.7	16.0
1988	100.1	29.6	0.6	5.3	23.7	8.7	15.0	70.5	2.5	68.0	169.6	61.9	90.2	17.5
1989	97.8	29.1	0.7	5.4	23.0	8.3	14.7	68.7	2.7	66.0	169.9	56.4	94.4	19.2
1990	93.4	29.6	0.6	5.7	23.3	7.9	15.4	63.8	3.1	60.7	161.0	53.8	86.7	20.5
1991	95.3	32.2	0.9	5.9	25.5	8.0	17.5	63.1	2.4	60.6	166.4	53.9	90.4	22.2
1992	91.2	32.1	0.7	5.9	25.5	9.0	16.5	59.2	2.3	56.8	152.2	48.9	83.2	20.1

Appendix 3:
Rate of Sentenced Prisoners
in State and Federal Institutions
from 1972 to 1992

Rate (per 100,000 resident population) of sentenced prisoners in State and Federal institutions on Dec. 31

By region and jurisdiction, 1972-92

Region and jurisdiction	1972	1973	1974	1975	1976	1977	1978	1979	1980	1981	1982	1983	1984	1985	1986	1987	1988	1989	1990	1991	1992
United States, total	94.6	97.8	103.6	113	123	129	135	136	139	153	170	179	188	200	216	228	244	271	292	310	330
Federal institutions, total	10.5	10.9	10.6	11	13	13	12	10	9	10	10	11	12	14	15	16	17	19	20	22	26
State institutions, total	84.1	86.8	93.0	102	111	116	123	126	130	144	160	167	176	187	201	211	227	253	272	287	305
Northeast	56.8	60.4	63.4	70	73	77	82	84	87	103	115	127	136	145	157	169	186	215	232	248	261
Connecticut	59.3	54.2	47.6	59	62	53	70	69	68	95	114	114	119	127	135	144	146	194	238	263	268
Maine	46.3	43.8	50.4	60	57	61	53	58	61	71	69	75	72	83	106	106	100	116	118	123	121
Massachusetts	32.1	34.3	38.4	42	46	48	49	50	56	65	77	79	84	88	92	102	109	122	132	143	161
New Hampshire	30.8	34.8	27.1	31	30	26	32	35	35	42	47	50	57	68	76	81	93	103	117	132	160
New Jersey	72.4	73.5	71.6	77	78	78	74	76	76	92	107	136	138	149	157	177	219	251	271	301	290
New York	64.0	71.4	78.5	89	98	108	114	120	123	145	158	172	187	195	216	229	248	285	304	320	340
Pennsylvania	52.6	55.0	56.9	60	56	56	65	67	68	78	88	98	109	119	128	136	149	169	183	192	207
Rhode Island	36.1	43.2	48.7	41	53	56	56	63	65	72	82	92	92	99	103	100	118	146	157	173	170
Vermont	30.0	40.3	51.5	51	64	57	76	62	67	76	84	72	74	82	81	91	98	109	117	124	151
Midwest	65.6	62.8	69.0	84	95	108	104	105	109	121	130	135	144	161	173	184	200	225	239	255	273
Illinois	50.4	50.3	55.9	73	87	95	96	95	94	113	119	135	149	161	168	171	181	211	234	247	271
Indiana	72.8	63.4	57.5	73	79	80	82	98	114	138	152	164	165	175	181	192	202	217	223	226	242
Iowa	45.5	49.0	51.6	63	66	70	70	72	86	88	93	92	97	98	98	101	107	126	139	144	160
Kansas	73.5	60.6	63.5	76	91	97	98	95	106	116	129	152	173	192	217	233	232	222	227	231	238
Michigan	93.9	86.8	94.6	119	137	151	162	163	163	165	162	159	161	196	227	259	298	340	366	388	413
Minnesota	34.5	36.0	35.1	42	41	44	41	51	49	49	50	52	52	56	58	60	64	71	72	78	85
Missouri	74.7	79.4	88.0	92	105	111	116	113	112	131	147	162	175	194	203	218	236	269	287	305	311
Nebraska	62.8	66.0	67.9	80	93	83	80	71	89	104	99	91	95	108	116	123	129	141	140	145	151
North Dakota	28.8	24.9	20.7	27	26	30	21	19	28	33	47	51	54	55	53	57	62	62	67	68	67
Ohio	77.2	71.9	86.9	107	117	120	122	125	125	139	160	155	174	194	209	219	243	279	289	324	347
South Dakota	51.0	34.9	37.0	49	70	76	74	77	88	97	109	115	127	146	160	160	143	175	187	191	208
Wisconsin	44.9	47.2	56.4	65	71	72	73	73	85	93	96	102	105	113	119	126	130	138	149	157	176

South	124.5	128.3	135.0	150	161	169	181	196	188	201	224	225	231	236	248	255	266	292	316	333	355
Alabama	103.5	104.5	110.3	121	83	94	144	141	149	183	215	243	256	267	283	307	300	328	370	394	407
Arkansas	80.4	82.2	99.6	102	115	111	115	132	128	143	166	179	188	195	198	227	230	261	277	317	340
Delaware	49.3	57.1	76.1	100	118	120	173	181	183	208	250	273	263	281	311	326	331	333	323	344	390
District of Columbia	340.8	324.2	289.2	326	334	330	383	433	426	467	531	558	649	738	753	905	1,078	1,132	1,148	1,221	1,287
Florida	139.3	132.5	137.9	183	211	221	239	220	208	224	261	235	242	247	272	265	278	307	336	344	355
Georgia	174.3	173.3	191.4	204	225	224	216	224	219	220	247	259	254	251	265	282	281	300	327	342	365
Kentucky	89.5	89.4	91.7	100	107	106	97	105	99	114	110	127	128	133	142	147	191	222	241	262	274
Louisiana	92.2	108.3	127.7	126	120	152	184	190	211	216	251	290	310	308	316	346	370	396	427	462	484
Maryland	139.3	144.0	155.0	169	192	198	193	187	183	218	244	277	285	279	280	282	291	323	348	366	381
Mississippi	83.1	75.5	91.8	103	91	67	110	141	132	177	210	211	229	237	249	256	277	293	307	330	327
North Carolina	159.9	183.9	207.2	210	214	234	223	240	244	248	255	233	246	254	257	250	249	250	265	269	290
Oklahoma	139.7	120.4	108.5	114	133	129	146	147	151	169	201	212	236	250	288	296	323	361	381	416	459
South Carolina	121.2	130.1	158.4	198	230	239	243	237	238	251	270	276	284	294	324	344	369	416	451	473	486
Tennessee	81.9	84.2	90.9	109	114	127	134	151	153	171	173	187	154	149	157	156	157	213	207	227	234
Texas	136.0	146.6	140.6	154	167	176	189	196	210	210	237	221	226	226	228	231	240	257	290	297	344
Virginia	106.3	107.9	105.1	110	126	142	157	158	165	177	185	204	215	217	215	217	230	263	279	311	327
West Virginia	59.1	60.8	57.3	65	71	67	63	66	64	80	77	83	82	89	77	77	78	84	85	83	92
West	78.6	8.6	93.9	84	91	92	99	101	105	119	139	152	166	176	197	214	234	256	277	287	299
Alaska	61.0	56.3	57.1	56	63	75	127	133	143	170	194	219	252	288	306	339	355	361	348	345	327
Arizona	76.9	81.0	97.0	118	125	129	146	139	160	184	209	223	247	256	268	307	328	350	375	396	409
California	83.9	96.7	105.6	81	85	80	88	93	98	114	135	150	162	181	212	231	257	283	311	318	339
Colorado	81.3	77.5	79.4	80	87	89	93	90	96	92	108	109	104	103	115	145	174	207	209	249	256
Hawaii	38.8	37.3	38.6	42	39	44	57	58	65	77	88	103	124	134	142	141	136	142	150	153	164
Idaho	49.6	54.6	65.5	71	82	87	91	92	87	99	107	121	127	133	142	144	157	180	190	205	209
Montana	39.5	43.5	45.6	50	73	81	87	96	94	104	114	104	121	136	135	147	158	165	176	183	180
Nevada	121.2	134.9	130.3	136	156	187	204	224	230	245	301	354	380	397	447	432	452	438	444	439	448
New Mexico	55.7	66.4	80.7	86	105	126	123	112	106	100	126	142	133	144	154	174	180	178	196	191	197
Oregon	84.4	74.7	88.3	108	122	122	117	122	120	124	146	157	170	165	176	200	215	235	223	228	174
Utah	51.2	44.7	46.1	54	60	64	69	68	64	73	77	84	98	108	110	115	124	137	142	149	146
Washington	77.1	77.1	86.2	96	109	118	122	113	106	125	148	155	156	156	147	134	124	142	162	182	192
Wyoming	75.7	76.6	73.9	80	87	98	102	95	113	117	135	138	143	148	168	190	199	216	237	237	226

Appendix 4:
Data on Social Variables Used in
The Politics of Prision Expansion

(List of Seventeen Variables, List of States in Order of Imprisonment Increase and Data for Seventeen Variables in Each State)

VARIABLE 1:   Percent increase in the imprisonment rate in that state
               between 1972 and 1992

VARIABLE 2:   Percent increase in <u>Uniform Crime Reports</u> (<u>UCR</u>) rate in
               that state between 1972 and 1992

VARIABLE 3:   Imprisonment rate per 100,000 population in 1972

VARIABLE 4:   Imprisonment rate per 100,000 population in 1992

VARIABLE 5:   <u>UCR</u> crime rate for 1972

VARIABLE 6:   <u>UCR </u>crime rate for 1992

VARIABLE 7:   Percent of the population that was African American in
               1990

VARIABLE 8:   Average per capita income

VARIABLE 9:   Percent of the population that is living below the pov-
               erty level

VARIABLE 10:   unemployment rate

VARIABLE 11:   Rate of drug arrests per 100,000 population

VARIABLE 12:   Homicide rate

VARIABLE 13:   Population in 1990

VARIABLE 14:   Population in 1970

VARIABLE 15:   Percent of the population that was African American in
               1970

VARIABLE 16:   Homicide rate in 1972

VARIABLE 17:   Average per capita income in 1970

* COLUMN ONE REPRESENT THE FIFTY STATES IN THE ORDER OF THE
INCREASE IN IMPRISONMENT RATE BETWEEN 1972 AND 1992

1. DELAWARE
2. ALASKA
3. ILLINOIS
4. ARIZONA
5. NEW YORK
6. LOUISIANA
7. NEW HAMPSHIRE
8. VERMONT
9. MASSACHUSETTS
10. RHODE ISLAND
11. MONTANA
12. OHIO
13. CONNECTICUT
14. MISSISSIPPI
15. HAWAII
16. ARKANSAS
17. IDAHO
18. MICHIGAN
19. SOUTH DAKOTA
20. CALIFORNIA
21. NEW JERSEY
22. SOUTH CAROLINA
23. MISSISSIPPI
24. ALABAMA
25. PENNSYLVANIA
26. WISCONSIN
27. NEVADA
28. NEW MEXICO
29. IOWA
30. INDIANA
31. OKLAHOMA
32. KANSAS
33. COLORADO
34. KENTUCKY
35. VIRGINIA
36. WYOMING
37. TENNESSEE
38. UTAH
39. MARYLAND
40. MAINE
41. TEXAS
42. FLORIDA
43. MINNESOTA
44. NEBRASKA
45. WASHINGTON
46. NORTH DAKOTA
47. GEORGIA
48. OREGON
49. NORTH CAROLINA
50. WEST VIRGINIA

	var00001	var00002	var00003	var00004	var00005	var00006	var00007	var00008
1	690.00	7.00	49.30	390.00	4523.00	4848.00	16.80	15.80
2	435.00	24.00	61.00	327.00	4478.00	5569.00	4.00	17.60
3	435.00	52.00	50.40	271.00	3791.00	5765.00	14.80	15.20
4	430.00	18.00	76.90	409.00	5933.00	7028.00	3.00	13.40
5	430.00	38.00	64.00	340.00	4231.00	5858.00	15.80	16.50
6	423.00	93.00	92.20	484.00	3382.00	6546.00	30.80	10.60
7	420.00	54.00	30.80	160.00	1991.00	3080.00	.60	15.90
8	401.00	54.00	30.00	151.00	2204.00	3410.00	.30	13.50
9	400.00	21.00	32.10	161.00	4107.00	5002.00	4.90	17.20
10	370.00	5.00	36.10	170.00	4553.00	4578.00	3.80	14.90
11	355.00	43.00	39.50	180.00	3205.00	4596.00	.30	11.20
12	350.00	35.00	77.20	347.00	3439.00	4665.00	10.60	13.40
13	345.00	42.00	59.30	268.00	3403.00	4848.00	8.30	20.10
14	340.00	4.00	93.90	413.00	5383.00	5810.00	13.90	14.00
15	325.00	32.00	38.80	164.00	4612.00	6112.00	2.40	15.70
16	325.00	119.00	80.40	340.00	2166.00	4761.00	15.90	10.50
17	320.00	16.00	49.80	209.00	3420.00	3996.00	.30	11.40
18	320.00	29.00	74.70	311.00	3933.00	5097.00	11.40	12.90
19	305.00	40.00	51.00	208.00	2127.00	2998.00	.40	10.80
20	305.00	5.00	83.90	339.00	6413.00	6679.00	7.40	16.40
21	301.00	31.00	72.40	290.00	3840.00	5084.00	13.40	18.70
22	300.00	80.00	121.20	486.00	3264.00	5893.00	29.80	11.80
23	295.00	137.00	83.10	327.00	1805.00	4282.00	35.50	9.60
24	294.00	126.00	103.50	407.00	2326.00	5268.00	25.20	11.40
25	293.00	43.00	52.60	207.00	2369.00	3392.00	9.10	14.00
26	290.00	46.00	44.90	176.00	2950.00	4319.00	5.00	13.20
27	270.00	6.00	121.20	448.00	5850.00	6203.00	6.50	15.20
28	263.00	36.00	55.70	197.00	4723.00	6434.00	1.90	11.20
29	251.00	56.00	45.50	160.00	2431.00	3957.00	1.70	12.40
30	235.00	45.00	72.80	242.00	3231.00	4686.00	7.80	13.10
31	228.00	74.00	139.70	459.00	3105.00	6431.00	7.40	11.80

	var00001	var00002	var00003	var00004	var00005	var00006	var00007	var00008
32	225.00	56.00	73.50	238.00	3404.00	5319.00	5.70	13.30
33	215.00	6.00	81.30	256.00	5593.00	5968.00	4.00	14.80
34	210.00	44.00	89.50	274.00	2233.00	3223.00	7.10	11.10
35	207.00	39.00	106.30	327.00	3081.00	4298.00	18.80	15.70
36	200.00	48.00	75.70	226.00	3082.00	4575.00	.80	12.30
37	185.00	94.00	81.90	234.00	2646.00	5135.00	16.90	12.20
38	185.00	34.00	51.20	146.00	4206.00	5858.00	.60	11.00
39	175.00	34.00	139.30	381.00	4628.00	6224.00	24.90	17.70
40	162.00	51.00	46.30	121.00	2320.00	3523.00	.40	12.90
41	153.00	83.00	136.00	344.00	3839.00	7057.00	11.90	12.90
42	155.00	55.00	139.30	365.00	5376.00	8358.00	13.60	14.60
43	150.00	29.00	34.50	86.00	3554.00	4590.00	2.10	14.30
44	140.00	64.00	62.80	151.00	2628.00	4324.00	3.60	12.40
45	130.00	46.00	28.80	67.00	1987.00	2903.00	2.60	11.00
46	110.00	109.00	174.30	365.00	3051.00	6405.00	.50	13.60
47	105.00	15.00	84.40	174.00	5048.00	5820.00	26.90	13.40
48	82.00	118.00	159.90	290.00	2659.00	5802.00	1.60	12.80
49	65.00	81.00	59.10	92.00	1435.00	2609.00	21.90	10.50
50	50.00	31.00	77.10	192.00	4706.00	6172.00	3.00	14.90

	var00009	var00010	var00011	var00012	var00013	var00014	var00015	var00016
1	8.70	5.20	334.00	5.00	.66	.55	14.10	6.90
2	9.00	7.00	101.00	9.00	.55	.30	.66	9.50
3	11.90	6.10	101.00	7.40	11.43	11.11	12.76	8.80
4	15.70	5.30	383.00	8.60	3.66	1.77	2.90	7.30
5	13.00	5.20	683.00	13.30	17.99	18.23	11.89	11.00
6	23.60	6.20	309.00	20.30	4.21	3.64	29.31	13.20
7	6.40	5.70	162.00	2.00	1.10	.74	.33	1.70
8	9.90	4.80	86.00	3.60	.56	.44	.46	1.70
9	8.90	5.90	254.00	3.90	6.01	6.88	3.10	3.70
10	9.60	6.70	281.00	3.90	1.00	.96	2.60	1.30
11	16.10	5.70	129.00	3.00	.80	.69	.28	2.50
12	12.50	5.60	91.00	6.00	10.84	10.65	9.14	7.50
13	6.80	5.00	571.00	6.30	3.28	3.03	6.97	3.20
14	13.10	7.50	297.00	9.80	5.11	4.67	10.27	8.30
15	8.30	2.70	325.00	3.60	1.10	.77	2.50	6.80
16	19.10	6.80	256.00	10.20	2.35	1.92	18.30	10.40
17	13.30	5.80	175.00	2.90	1.00	.71	.33	3.80
18	13.30	5.70	269.00	11.30	9.29	8.87	9.90	11.00
19	15.90	3.60	61.00	3.40	.70	.67	.35	1.20
20	12.50	5.60	839.00	13.10	29.70	19.96	7.00	8.80
21	7.60	4.90	600.00	5.30	7.73	7.16	10.70	6.80
22	15.40	4.70	430.00	10.30	3.48	2.59	30.40	16.80
23	25.20	7.40	178.00	13.50	2.57	2.21	36.90	15.40
24	18.30	6.70	188.00	11.60	4.04	3.44	26.20	14.10
25	11.10	5.30	233.00	6.80	11.88	11.79	8.60	3.00
26	10.70	4.30	192.00	4.40	4.89	4.41	2.90	2.80
27	6.40	5.70	560.00	10.40	1.20	.49	5.70	13.50
28	20.60	6.20	220.00	8.00	1.51	1.01	1.90	11.10
29	11.50	4.20	116.00	2.30	2.77	2.82	1.10	1.70
30	10.70	5.30	110.00	7.50	5.54	5.19	6.80	6.00
31	16.70	5.50	284.00	8.40	3.14	2.55	6.70	7.00

	var00009	var00010	var00011	var00012	var00013	var00014	var00015	var00016
32	11.50	4.30	223.00	6.40	2.47	2.24	4.70	4.00
33	11.70	4.90	228.00	5.80	3.29	2.20	3.00	8.30
34	19.00	5.80	315.00	6.80	3.80	3.21	7.10	9.80
35	10.20	4.20	285.00	8.30	6.18	4.84	18.50	9.80
36	11.90	5.20	121.00	3.40	.46	.33	.61	4.10
37	15.70	5.20	241.00	10.20	4.87	3.92	15.80	11.20
38	11.40	4.20	190.00	3.10	1.72	1.05	.19	2.90
39	8.30	4.60	599.00	12.70	4.78	3.92	17.80	12.50
40	10.80	5.20	187.00	1.60	1.22	.99	.21	3.20
41	18.10	6.10	366.00	11.90	16.96	11.19	12.50	12.30
42	12.70	5.90	606.00	8.90	12.93	6.78	15.30	12.70
43	10.20	4.80	126.00	3.40	4.37	3.80	.09	2.40
44	11.10	2.10	263.00	3.90	1.57	1.48	2.70	2.90
45	14.40	4.00	66.00	5.20	4.86	3.40	.21	4.20
46	14.70	5.40	272.00	1.70	.64	.62	.38	1.30
47	12.40	5.50	346.00	11.40	6.47	4.58	25.90	18.50
48	13.00	4.00	376.00	4.60	2.84	2.09	1.20	5.50
49	19.70	8.20	88.00	11.30	6.62	5.06	22.20	13.50
50	10.90	4.80	220.00	6.90	1.79	1.74	3.80	5.10

	var00017
1	4483.00
2	4603.00
3	4492.00
4	3631.00
5	4714.00
6	3068.00
7	3745.00
8	3311.00
9	4340.00
10	3941.00
11	3498.00
12	3992.00
13	4871.00
14	3768.00
15	4562.00
16	2869.00
17	3280.00
18	4156.00
19	3124.00
20	4467.00
21	4635.00
22	2963.00
23	2596.00
24	2913.00
25	3943.00
26	3794.00
27	4452.00
28	3117.00
29	3749.00
30	3752.00
31	3350.00

	var00017
32	3841.00
33	3639.00
34	3104.00
35	3653.00
36	3796.00
37	3062.00
38	3228.00
39	4281.00
40	3272.00
41	3576.00
42	3692.00
43	3848.00
44	3794.00
45	4022.00
46	3120.00
47	3318.00
48	3694.00
49	3218.00
50	3047.00

Appendix 5:
Multiple Regression of
Selected Variables

Equation Number 1   Dependent Variable   PRISINCP

Multiple R   .48891
R Square   .23903
Adjusted R Square   .18941
Standard Error   109.90974

Analysis of Variance
                  DF   Sum of Squares   Mean Square
Regression   3   174551.36219   58183.78740
Residual   46   555686.95781   12080.15126

F =   4.81648   Signif F = .0053

----------------- Variables in the Equation -----------------

Variable   B   SE B   Beta   T   Sig T

PRISON72   -1.733684   .481660   -.503907   -3.599   .0008
BLACK70P   2.000443   1.837247   .152249   1.089   .2819
BLACKINC   -.068750   .037348   -.249339   -1.841   .0721
(Constant) 397.292856   40.189633   9.885   .0000

                PRISINCP   PRISON72   PRISON92   BLACK70P   BLACK90P   BLACKINC

PRISINCP   1.0000   -.3852   .3083   .0378   .0799   -.1572
              (50)   (50)   (50)   (50)   (50)   (50)
               P= .   P= .006   P= .029   P= .795   P= .581   P= .276

PRISON72   -.3852   1.0000   .7002   .3538   .3405   -.2602
              (50)   (50)   (50)   (50)   (50)   (50)
               P= .006   P= .   P= .000   P= .012   P= .016   P= .068

PRISON92   .3083   .7002   1.0000   .4961   .5118   -.3261
              (50)   (50)   (50)   (50)   (50)   (50)
               P= .029   P= .000   P= .   P= .000   P= .000   P= .021

BLACK70P   .0378   .3538   .4961   1.0000   .9853   -.2558
              (50)   (50)   (50)   (50)   (50)   (50)
               P= .795   P= .012   P= .000   P= .   P= .000   P= .073

BLACK90P   .0799   .3405   .5118   .9853   1.0000   -.2165
              (50)   (50)   (50)   (50)   (50)   (50)
               P= .581   P= .016   P= .000   P= .000   P= .   P= .131

BLACKINC   -.1572   -.2602   -.3261   -.2558   -.2165   1.0000
              (50)   (50)   (50)   (50)   (50)   (50)
               P= .276   P= .068   P= .021   P= .073   P= .131   P= .

140

HOM72	-.0640	.4601	.5418	.8270	.8191	-.1895
	(50)	(50)	(50)	(50)	(50)	(50)
	P= .659	P= .001	P= .000	P= .000	P= .000	P= .187
HOM92	.0567	.4031	.6097	.7668	.7849	-.1678
	(50)	(50)	(50)	(50)	(50)	(50)
	P= .696	P= .004	P= .000	P= .000	P= .000	P= .244
HOMINC	.1498	-.2755	-.1970	-.2939	-.2781	.0505
	(50)	(50)	(50)	(50)	(50)	(50)
	P= .299	P= .053	P= .170	P= .038	P= .051	P= .728
UCR72	.1734	.1702	.3332	-.0934	-.0455	-.0320
	(50)	(50)	(50)	(50)	(50)	(50)
	P= .229	P= .237	P= .018	P= .519	P= .754	P= .826
UCR92	-.0194	.5675	.5678	.1733	.1806	-.1419
	(50)	(50)	(50)	(50)	(50)	(50)
	P= .894	P= .000	P= .000	P= .229	P= .209	P= .326
CRIMINCP	-.2685	.4015	.1816	.4484	.3714	-.1423
	(50)	(50)	(50)	(50)	(50)	(50)
	P= .059	P= .004	P= .207	P= .001	P= .008	P= .324

	HOM72	HOM92	HOMINC	UCR72	UCR92	CRIMINCP
PRISINCP	-.0640	.0567	.1498	.1734	-.0194	-.2685
	(50)	(50)	(50)	(50)	(50)	(50)
	P= .659	P= .696	P= .299	P= .229	P= .894	P= .059
PRISON72	.4601	.4031	-.2755	.1702	.5675	.4015
	(50)	(50)	(50)	(50)	(50)	(50)
	P= .001	P= .004	P= .053	P= .237	P= .000	P= .004
PRISON92	.5418	.6097	-.1970	.3332	.5678	.1816
	(50)	(50)	(50)	(50)	(50)	(50)
	P= .000	P= .000	P= .170	P= .018	P= .000	P= .207
BLACK7GP	.8270	.7668	-.2939	-.0934	.1733	.4484
	(50)	(50)	(50)	(50)	(50)	(50)
	P= .000	P= .000	P= .038	P= .519	P= .229	P= .001
BLACK90P	.8191	.7849	-.2781	-.0455	.1806	.3714
	(50)	(50)	(50)	(50)	(50)	(50)
	P= .000	P= .000	P= .051	P= .754	P= .209	P= .008
BLACKINC	-.1895	-.1678	.0505	-.0320	-.1419	-.1423
	(50)	(50)	(50)	(50)	(50)	(50)
	P= .187	P= .244	P= .728	P= .826	P= .326	P= .324
HOM72	1.0000	.8368	-.5261	.2222	.4069	.2205
	(50)	(50)	(50)	(50)	(50)	(50)
	P= .	P= .000	P= .000	P= .121	P= .003	P= .124

HOM92	.8368	1.0000	-.1657	.2261	.4215	.2282
	(50)	(50)	(50)	(50)	(50)	(50)
	P= .000	P= .	P= .250	P= .114	P= .002	P= .111
HOMINC	-.5261	-.1657	1.0000	-.1056	-.2332	-.1107
	(50)	(50)	(50)	(50)	(50)	(50)
	P= .000	P= .250	P= .	P= .465	P= .103	P= .444
UCR72	.2222	.2261	-.1056	1.0000	.7595	-.6549
	(50)	(50)	(50)	(50)	(50)	(50)
	P= .121	P= .114	P= .465	P= .	P= .000	P= .000
UCR92	.4069	.4215	-.2332	.7595	1.0000	-.0549
	(50)	(50)	(50)	(50)	(50)	(50)
	P= .003	P= .002	P= .103	P= .000	P= .	P= .705
CRIMINCP	.2205	.2282	-.1107	-.6549	-.0549	1.0000
	(50)	(50)	(50)	(50)	(50)	(50)
	P= .124	P= .111	P= .444	P= .000	P= .705	P= .

Number of valid observations (listwise) =   50.00

Variable	Mean	Std.Dev.	Minimum	Maximum	N
DRUGP92	276.52	171.25	61.00	839.00	50
POV92	12.99	4.22	6.40	25.20	50
PRISINCP	271.86	109.16	15.00	690.00	50

	DRUGP92	POV92	PRISINCP
DRUGP92	1.000	-.1858	.0692
	(50)	(50)	(50)
	p=.000	p=.196	P=.633
POVP92	-.1858	1.000	-.1355
	(50)	(50)	(50)
	p=.196	p=.000	P=.368
PRISINCP	.0692	-.1355	1.000
	(50)	(50)	(50)
	p=.633	p=.368	p=000

142

Appendix 6:
Bivariate Correlation of
Selected Variables

```
                Correlation Coefficients

                VAR 1       VAR 8

VAR 1        1.0000       .2841
             (    50)     (   50)
                          p=.046

VAR 8          .2841     1.0000
             (    50)     (   50)
             p=.046


                VAR 1       VAR 9

VAR 1        1.0000      -.1400
             (    50)     (   50)
                          p=.332

VAR 9         -.1400     1.0000
             (    50)     (   50)
             p=.332


                VAR 1       VAR 11

VAR 1        1.0000       .0680
             (    50)     (   50)
                          p=.639

VAR 11         .0680     1.0000
             (    50)     (   50)
             p=.639


                VAR 1       VAR 10

VAR 1        1.0000       .1964
             (    50)     (   50)
                          p=.172

VAR 10         .1964     1.0000
             (    50)     (   50)
             p=.172
```

Selected Bibliography

Adamson, C. R. "Toward a Marxian Penology: Captive Criminal Populations as Economic Threats and Resources." *Social Problems* 31, No. 4 (1984): 435–458.

Archambeault, William G. "Impact of Computer Based Technologies on Criminal Justice." In Roslyn Muraskin and Albert R. Roberts, eds., *Visions for Change: Crime and Justice in the Twenty-First Century.* Upper Saddle River, N.J.: Prentice-Hall, 1996, pp. 299–315.

Austin, James, and John Irwin. *Who Goes to Prison?* San Francisco: National Council on Crime and Delinquency, 1991.

Barlow, David E., Melissa Hickman Barlow, and Theodore G. Chiricos. "Long Economic Cycles and the Criminal Justice System in the United States." *Crime, Law and Social Change: An International Journal* 19, No. 2 (March 1993): 143–168.

Barr, William P. "Speech to California's District Attorney's Association." *Federal Sentencing Reporter* 4, No. 6.

Becker, Gary S. "Crime and Punishment: An Economic Approach." *Journal of Political Economy* 76 (1968): 169–217.

Berk, Richard A., David Rauma, Sheldon L. Messinger, and Thomas F. Cooley. "A Test of the Stability of Punishment Hypothesis: The Case of California, 1851–1970." *American Sociological Review* 46 (1981): 805–829.

Blumstein, Alfred, "Prisons." in James Q. Wilson, and Joan Petersilia, eds., *Crime.* San Francisco: ICS Press, 1995, pp. 387–419.

Blumstein, Alfred, and Jacqueline Cohen. "A Theory of the Stability of Punishment." *Journal of Criminal Law and Criminology* 64 (1973): 198–207.

Blumstein, Alfred, J. Cohen, and D. Nagin. *Deterrence and Incapacitation: Estimating the Effects of Criminal Sanctions on Crime Rates.* Washington, D.C.: National Academy of Sciences, 1978, 42–44.

Blumstein, Alfred, Jacqueline Cohen, Daniel Nagin, and Soumyo Moitra. "On Testing the Stability of Punishment Hypothesis: A Reply." *Journal of Criminal Law and Criminology* 72, No. 4 (1981): 1799–1808.

Blumstein, Alfred, and Soumyo Moitra. "An Analysis of Time Series of the Imprisonment Rate in the States of the United States: A Further Test of the Stability of Punishment Hypothesis." *Journal of Criminal Law and Criminology* 70 (1979): 376–390.

Box, Steven, and Chris Hale. "Unemployment, Imprisonment and Prison Overcrowding." *Contemporary Crisis* 9 (1985): 209–228.

Braithwaite, John. "The Political Economy of Punishment." In E. L. Wheelwright and Ken Buckley, eds., *Essays in the Political Economy of Australian Capitalism*, Vol 4. Sydney, Australia: ANZ Books, 1980.

Carlson, Kenneth et al. *American Prisons and Jails*. Vol. 2, *Population Trends and Projections*. Washington, D.C.: National Institute of Justice and Abt Associates, 1980.

Carpenter, Alan, and Carl Provorse. *World Almanac of the United States*. Mahwah, N.J.: Funk and Wagnalls, 1993.

Chiricos, T. G. "Rates of Crime and Unemployment: An Analysis of Aggregate Research Evidence." *Social Problems* 34, No. 2 (April 1987): 187–212.

Chiricos, T. G., and W. D. Bales. "Unemployment and Punishment: An Empirical Assessment." *Criminology* 29, No. 4 (1991): 701–715.

Chiricos, T. G., and M. A. DeLone. "Labor Surplus and Punishment: A Review and Assessment of Theory and Evidence." *Social Problems* 39, No. 4 (1992): 421–433.

Christie, Nils. *Crime as Industry*. Oslo, Norway: Universitetflag, 1993.

Clarke, Steven. "Getting Them out of Circulation: Does Incapacitation of Juvenile Offenders Reduce Crime?" *Journal of Criminal Law and Criminology* 65 (1974): 528–535.

Clear, Todd R. *Harm in American Penology: Offenders, Victims and Their Communities*. Albany: State University of New York Press, 1994.

Clear, Todd R., and Anthony A. Braga. "Community Corrections." In James Q. Wilson and Joan Petersilia, eds., *Crime*. San Francisco: ICS Press, 1995, pp. 421–444.

Cohen, Robyn. *Prisoners in 1990*. Washington, D.C.: Bureau of Justice Statistics, 1991.

Cook, Philip. "Research in Criminal Deterrence: Laying the Groundwork for the Second Decade." In Norval Morris and Michael Tonry, eds., *Crime and Justice: An Annual Review of Research*, Vol. 2. Chicago: University of Chicago Press, 1979, pp. 211–268.

Cullen, Francis T., Gregory A. Clark, and John F. Wozniak. "Explaining the Get Tough Movement: Can the Public Be Blamed?" *Federal Probation* 49 (1985): 16–24.

Curley, Bob. "Corrections-Industrial Complex Feeds off War on Drugs." *Alcoholism and Drug Abuse Weekly* 1995 7, No. 43 (November 6, 1995), p. 5.

Currie, Elliot. *Confronting Crime: An American Challenge*. New York: Pantheon Books, 1985.

———. *Reckoning: Drugs, the Cities and the American Future*. New York: Hill and Wang, 1993.

Davey, Joseph Dillon. "Crime in America Is Less Than You Think." *Human Rights* 21, No. 2 (Spring 1994), p. 1.

DiIulio, John J., and Anne M. Diehl. "Does Prison Pay?" Princeton University Center of Domestic and Comparative Policy Studies, 1991. Unpublished manuscript.

Durkheim, Emile. "The Evolution of Punishment." 1900. Reprint. In S. Lukes and A. Scull, eds., *Durkheim and the Law*. New York: St. Martin's Press, 1983.

Elias, Robert. "Official Stories: Media Coverage of American Crime Policy." *The Humanist* 54, No. 1 (January–February) 1994: 3–8.

Erhlich, Isaac. "Participation in Illegitimate Activities: An Economic Analysis." In C. S. Becer and W. M. Landes, eds., *Essays in the Economics of Crime and Punishment*. New York: National Bureau of Economic Research, 1974.

Galliher, John F. *Criminology: Human Rights, Criminal Law and Crime*. Englewood Cliffs, N.J: Prentice-Hall, 1989.

Gans, Herbert. *The War against the Poor: The Underclass and Antipoverty Policy*. New York: Basic Books, 1995.

Gibbons, Don C. *Society, Crime and Criminal Behavior*. 6th ed. Englewood Cliffs, N.J.: Prentice-Hall, 1992.

Gordon, Dianna. *The Justice Juggernaut*. New Brunswick, N.J.: Rutgers University Press, 1991.

Grabosky, Peter N. "The Variability of Punishment." In Donald Black, ed., *Toward a General Theory of Social Control*, Vol. 1. Orlando, Fla.: Academic Press, 1984, pp. 121–147.

Greenberg, D. F. "The Dynamics of Oscillatory Punishment Processes." *Journal of Criminal Law and Criminology* 68 (1977): 643–651.

———. "The Incapacitative Effect of Imprisonment: Some Estimates." *Law and Society Review* 9 (Summer 1975): 541–580.

Greenwood, Peter, and Allan Abrahamse. *Selective Incapacitation*. Santa Monica, Calif.: RAND Corporation, 1952.

Harrison, Bennett, and Barry Bluestone, *The Great U-Turn*. New York: Basic Books, 1988.

Hirst, Paul Q. "Marx and Engels on Law, Crime and Morality." *Economy and Society* 1 (1972): 28–56.

Inciardi, James A. *Criminal Justice*. 5th ed. New York: Harcourt Brace College Publishers, 1996.

Inverarity, J., and D. McArthy. "Punishment and Social Structure Revisited: Unemployment and Imprisonment in the United States, 1948–1984." *Sociological Quarterly* 29 (1988): 263–279.

Jacob, Herbert. *The Frustration of Policy: Responses to Crime by American Cities*. Boston: Little, Brown, 1984.

Jacobs, David, and Ronald D. Helms. "Toward a Political Model of Incarceration: A Time-Series Examination of Multiple Explanations for Prison Admissions Rates." *American Journal of Sociology* 102, No. 2 (September 1996): 323–355.

Juzenas, Eric. "Prevention: Best Approach to Public Health Threat of Violence." *Nation's Health* 26 (Jan. 1, 1996).

Kizziah, Carol A. *The State of the Jails in California. Report No. 1: Overcrowding in the Jails*. Sacramento: California Board of Corrections, 1984.

Klofas, John. "The Jail and the Community." *Justice Quarterly* 7 (1990): 69–104.

LaFave, Wayne. *Arrest: The Decision to Take a Person into Custody.* Boston: Little, Brown, 1965.

P. J. Langan. "America's Soaring Prison Population." *Science* 251 (March 1991): 1570–1578.

Livingston, J. *Crime and Criminology.* Englewood Cliffs, N.J.: Prentice-Hall, 1992.

Lukes, Stephen. *Emile Durkheim: His Life and Work.* New York: Harper and Row, 1972.

Lynch, James. "Crime in International Perspective." In James Q. Wilson and Joan Petersilia, eds., *Crime.* San Francisco: ICS Press, 1995, pp. 11–38.

Melosi, Dario. "Georg Rusche and Otto Kirchheimer: *Punishment and Social Structure.*" *Crime and Social Justice* 9 (1978): 73–85.

———. "An Introduction: Fifty Years Later: *Punishment and Social Structure* in Comparative Analysis." *Contemporary Crisis* 13 (1989): 311–326.

Morris, Norval, and Gordon Hawkins. *The Honest Politician's Guide to Crime Control.* Chicago: University of Chicago Press, 1970.

Murray, Charles, and Louis A. Cox. *Beyond Probation: Juvenile Corrections and the Chronic Offender.* Beverley Hills, Calif.: Sage Publications, 1986.

National Institute on Drugs and Alcohol. *National Household Survey of Drug Abuse, Population Estimates, 1991.* Washington, D.C.: U.S. Government Printing Office, 1992.

"Periscope." *Newsweek.* June 10, 1996, p. 4.

Phillips, Kevin. *The Politics of Rich and Poor.* New York: Random House, 1990.

Piven, Frances Fox, and Richard Cloward. *Regulating the Poor.* New York: Vintage Books, 1993.

RAND Corporation. "California's New Three Strikes Law: Benefits, Costs and Alternatives." RAND Research Brief. Santa Monica, Calif.: RAND Corporation, 1994.

Rauma, David. "A Concluding Note on the Stability of Punishment: Reply to Blumstein, Cohen, Moitra, and Nagin." *Journal of Criminal Law and Criminology* 72, No. 4 (1981): 1809–1812.

Reiss, Albert J., and Jeffrey Roth, eds. *Understanding and Controlling Violence.* Washington, D.C.: National Academy Press, 1993.

Rubin, Sheldon. *Psychiatry and Criminal Law.* Dobbs Ferry, N.Y.: Oceana Publications, 1965.

Scheingold, Stuart A. "Politics, Public Policy and Street Crime." *Annals of the American Academy of Political and Social Science* 539 (May 1995): 155–168.

Silberman, Charles. *Criminal Violence, Criminal Justice.* New York: Random House, 1978.

Skogan, Wesley G. "Measurement Problems in Official and Survey Crime Rates." *Journal of Criminal Justice* 3 (1975): 17–32.

Skolnick, Jerome. "Wild Pitch: 'Three Strikes You're Out' and Other Bad Calls on Crime." *American Prospect* 17 (Spring 1994): 30–37.

Tonry, Michael. *Malign Neglect.* New York: Oxford University Press, 1995.

———. *Sentencing Matters.* New York: Oxford University Press, 1996.

Trebach, Arnold, and Eddy Engelsman. "Why Not Decriminalize?" *NPQ [New Perspective Quarterly]* (Summer 1989): 40–45.

U.S. Department of Justice. *Setting Prison Terms*. Washington, D.C.: Bureau of Justice Statistics, August 1983.

———. *Sourcebook of Criminal Justice Statistics, 1991*. Washington, D.C.: Bureau of Justice Statistics, 1992.

———. *Sourcebook of Criminal Justice Statistics, 1993*. Washington, D.C.: Bureau of Justice Statistics, 1994.

———. *Sourcebook of Criminal Justice Statistics, 1994*. Washington, D.C.: Bureau of Justice Statistics, 1995.

van Dijk, Jan, Pat Mayhew, and Martin Killias. *Experiences of Crime across the World*. Boston: Kluwer 1990.

Van Dine, Stephen, John Conrad, and Simon Dinitz. *Restraining the Wicked*. Lexington, Mass.: Lexington Books, 1979.

Welsh, Wayne N. "Jail Overcrowding and Court Ordered Reform." In Roslyn Muraskin and Albert R. Roberts, eds., *Visions for Change: Crime and Justice in the Twenty-First Century*. Upper Saddle River, N.J.: Prentice-Hall, 1996, pp. 199–211.

Welsh, Wayne N., Henry N. Pontell, Mathew C. Leone, and Patrick Kinkade. "Jail Overcrowding: An Analysis of Policy Makers' Perceptions." *Justice Quarterly* 7 (1990): 341–370.

Wilson, James Q. *Thinking about Crime*. New York: Basic Books, 1975.

Wilson, James Q., and Joan Petersilia, eds. *Crime*. San Francisco, ICS Press, 1995.

Zimring, Franklin E., and Gordon Hawkins. *Deterrence*. Chicago: University of Chicago Press, 1973.

———. *Incapacitation: Penal Confinement and the Restraint of Crime*. New York: Oxford University Press, 1995.

———. *Prison Population and Criminal Justice Policy in California*. Berkeley, Calif.: Institute of Governmental Studies Press, 1992.

———. *The Scale of Imprisonment*. Chicago: University of Chicago Press, 1991.

Index

About the Author

JOSEPH DILLON DAVEY is Professor of Political Science, Criminal Justice and Law at New England College. A lawyer as well as an author, Professor Davey has written extensively on the role of government in society, including *The New Social Contract: America's Journey from Welfare State to Police State* (Praeger, 1995).

ISBN 0-275-96209-1

EAN

9 780275 962098

HARDCOVER BAR CODE